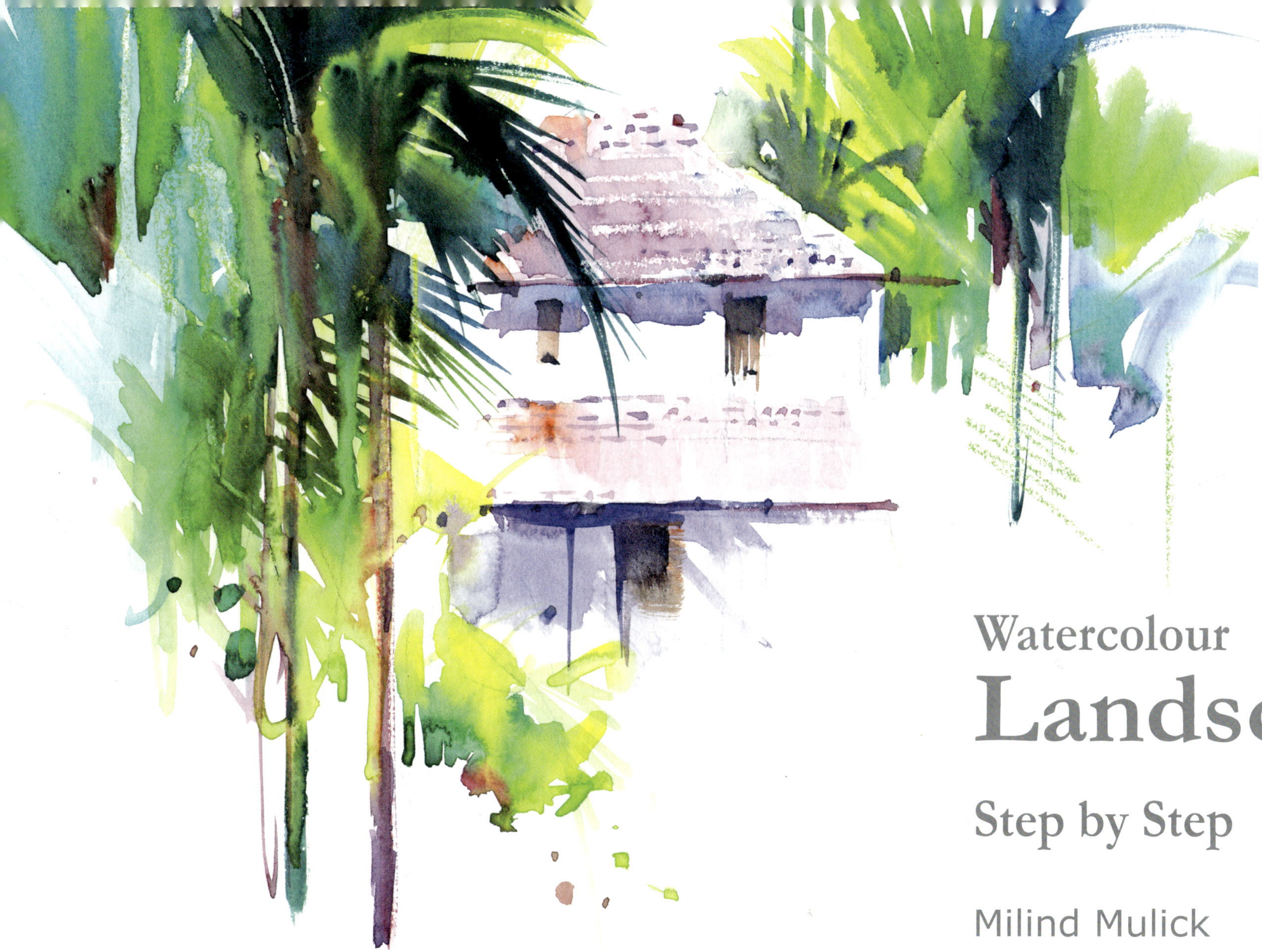

Watercolour Landscapes

Step by Step

Milind Mulick

JYOTSNA
PRAKASHAN

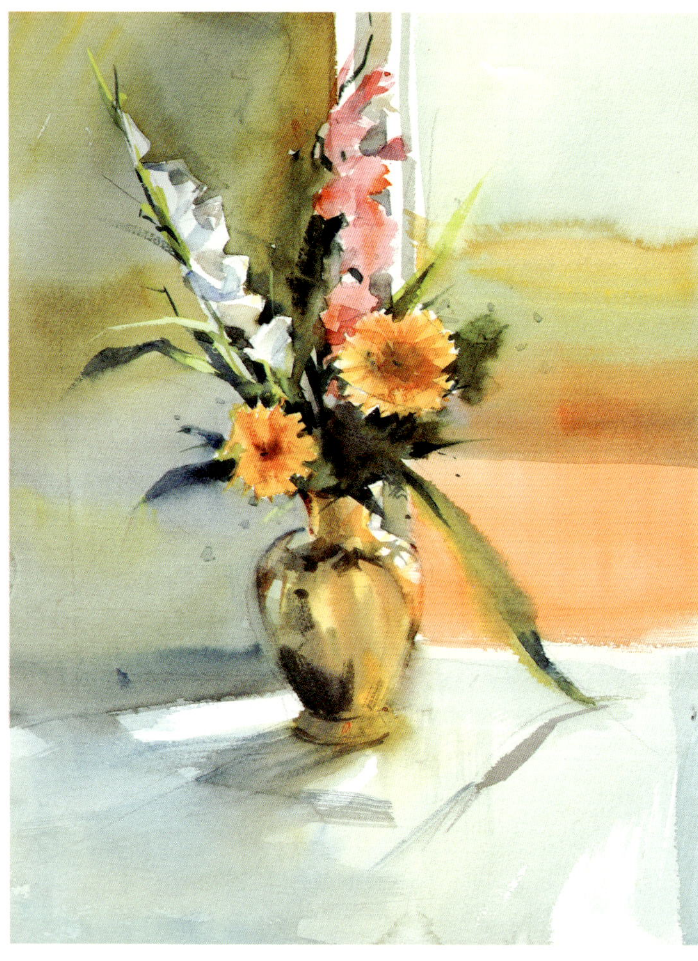

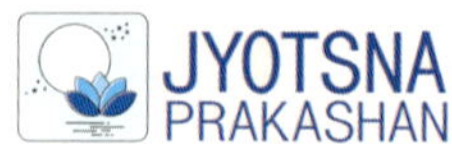

Watercolour Landscape Step by Step JP 233

Published by
Milind L. Paranjape,
Jyotsna Prakashan
430-31 Shaniwar Peth
Pune 411 030

Mumbai Office
Mohan Building,
162 JSS Marg, Girgaum,
Mumbai 400 004

First Edition : January 2010
Nineht Reprint : 2023

Editorial Assistance
Vilas Kulkarni

Translation
Dr. Ajey Hardeekar

Printed by : Imprint
133 Shaniwar Peth, Pune 411030

Price Rs. 350/-

ISBN 978-81-7925-395-3

Contents

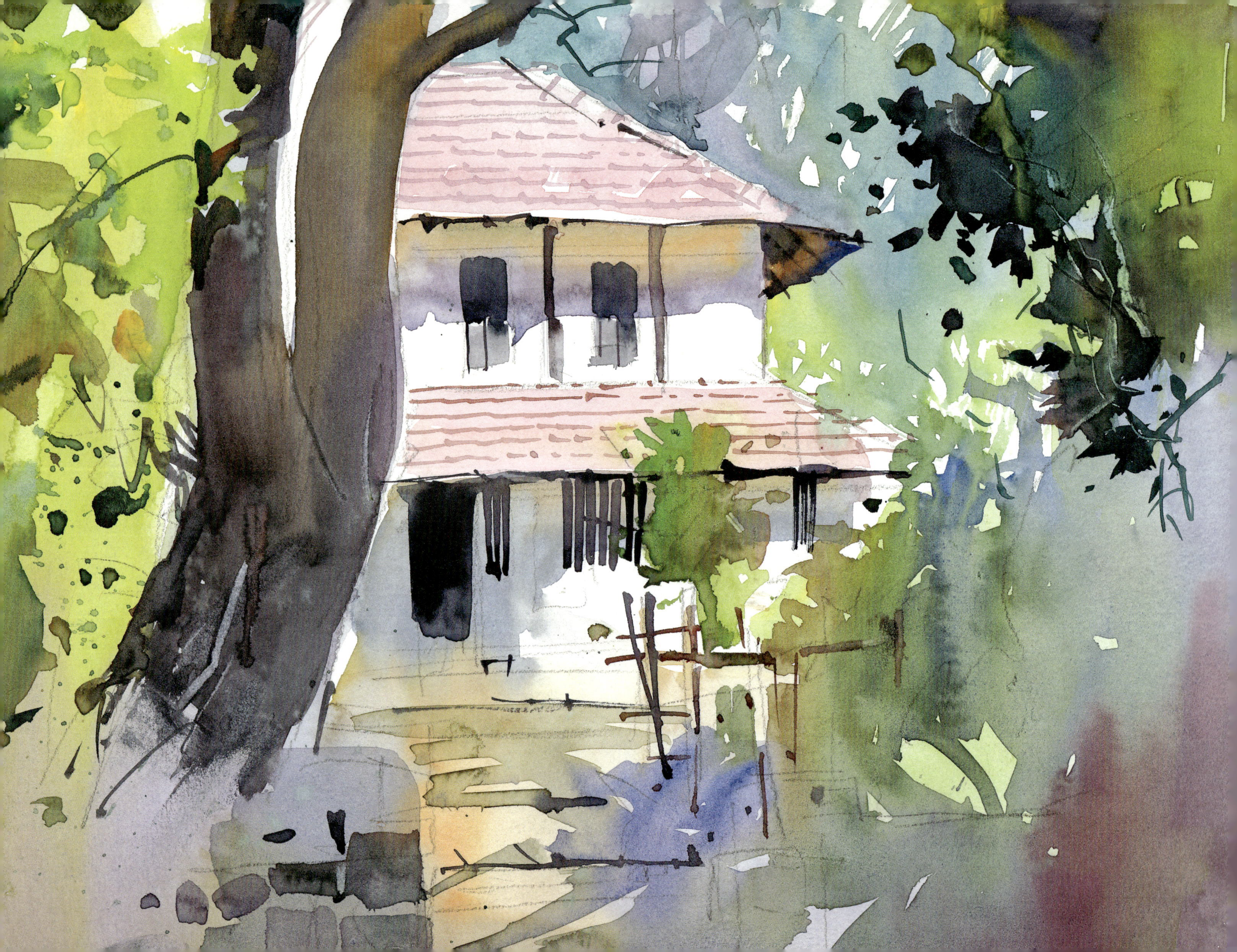

A Word or Two...

Watercolour landscapes have always evoked a sense of joy in the beholder. The bright, lucid colours and the way they seem to flow and blend on the paper transport the viewer to a different plane, even if for a few moments. Most of us who have seen the work of greats like Sargent, John Pike or Homer must have wondered whether we too would be able to paint like that! Those few who do try their hand at it often abandon their attempts after the inevitable initial failures. Yet I would appeal to all of you not to be so hasty. By learning a few simple techniques and practising diligently you too can paint well.

In this book I intend to present ten basic techniques along with demonstrations. Of course these are not like a magic wand that can instantly transform you into an accomplished watercolourist. But I assure you that you will certainly be able to start off on the right path towards acquiring the necessary skills.

So, come and join me on this exciting journey!

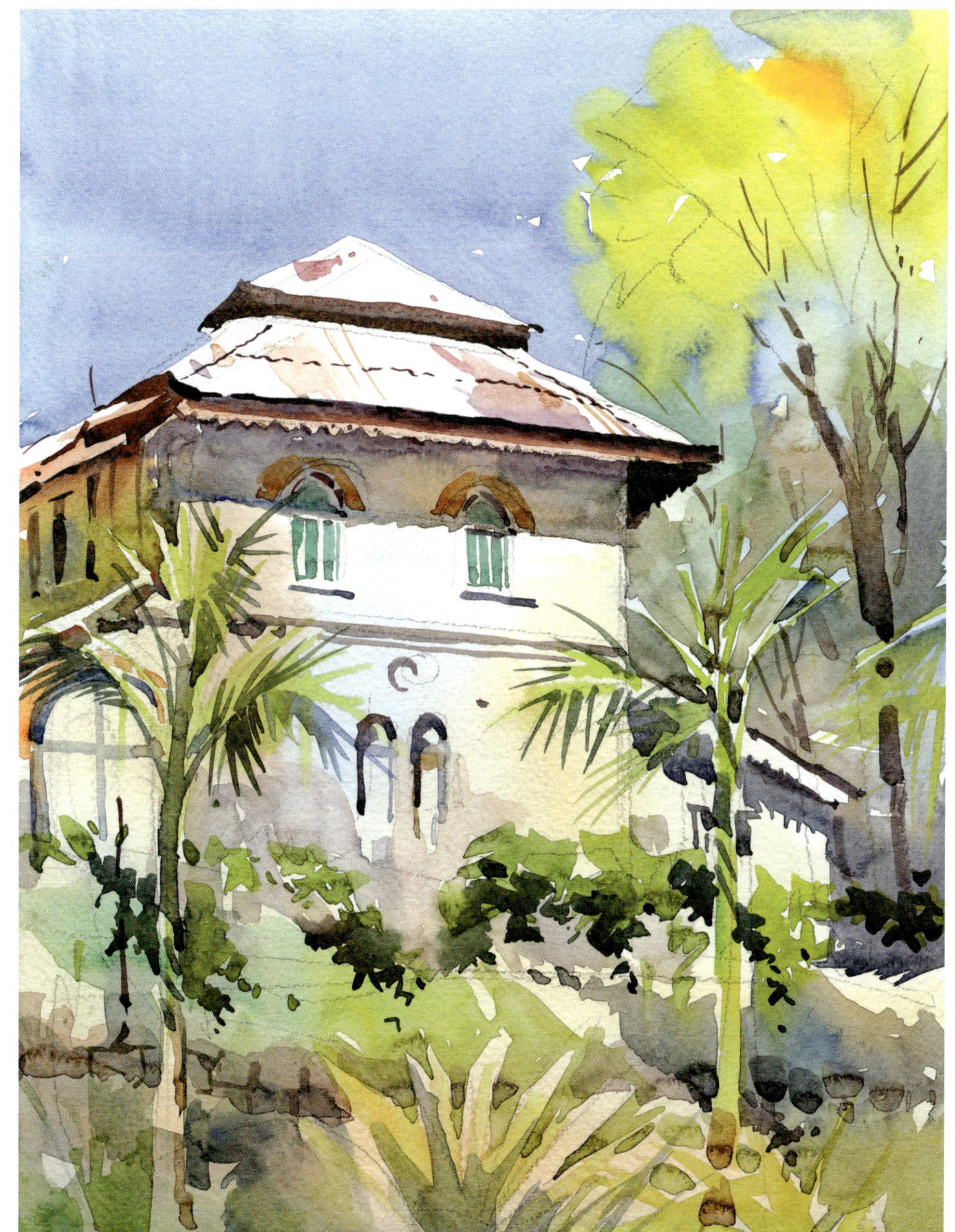

The Beginning...

If you were asked to describe in one word what 'watercolour' means to you, we would get different answers – transparency, brightness, flow, bold strokes, blending, simplicity – to name a few. All of these are characteristics of a good watercolour. I use the word 'good' because lightness, muddiness, thickness or uncontrolled colour mixing can also be characteristics, albeit 'bad' ones of a watercolour.

So, how does one avoid the pitfalls on the way to imbibing the techniques of painting a good watercolour? For this, I propose three simple 'rules' that you would need to keep in mind every time you pick up your paint brush and paper. These are:

1. Lots of water, lots of colour.
2. Dialogue.
3. Make mistakes!

1. Lots of water, lots of colour

Many of us have begun painting in our school days. We used to take very little paint onto our palette and mix little water into it. This was partly because paints have always been costly. However if we want transparency, brightness, flow and mixing of colours it is vital to mix up a lot of paint using a lot of water in readiness. Often we need to apply the second layer even before the first has dried. This would be impossible if we ran out of colour midway through. Also, unless we mix up a lot of paint at a time, we cannot maintain the exact shade we set out with. It becomes very difficult if we keep on opening the tubes every time we run out of colour. We also need to avoid formation of 'edges' when a different colour is applied. These edges are absolutely against the 'flowing' nature of a watercolour. So it is better to make it a habit to mix a lot of water when we prepare our palette.

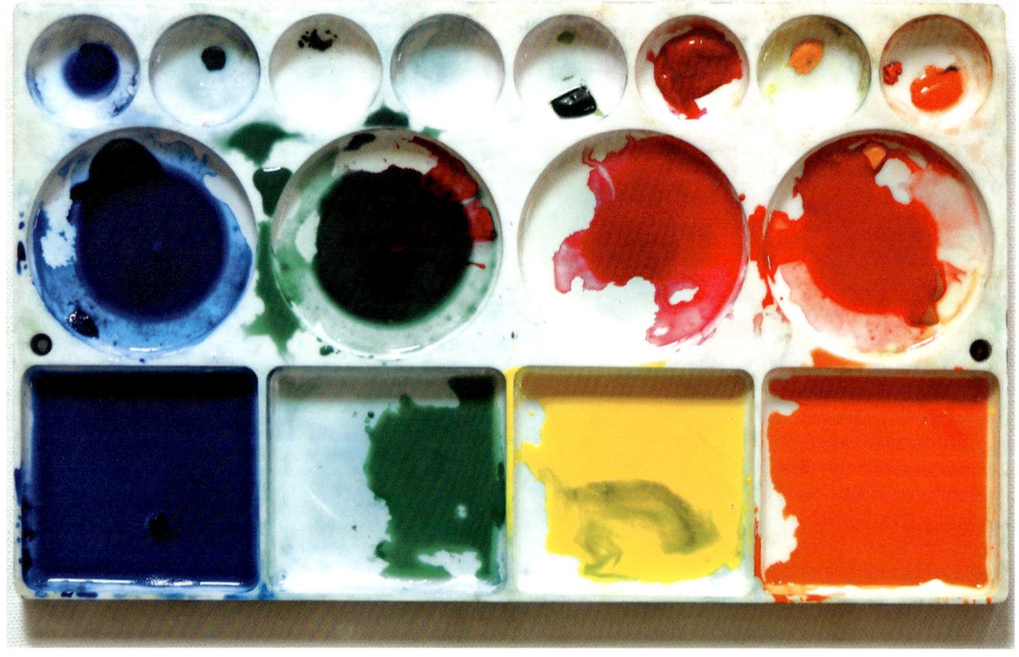

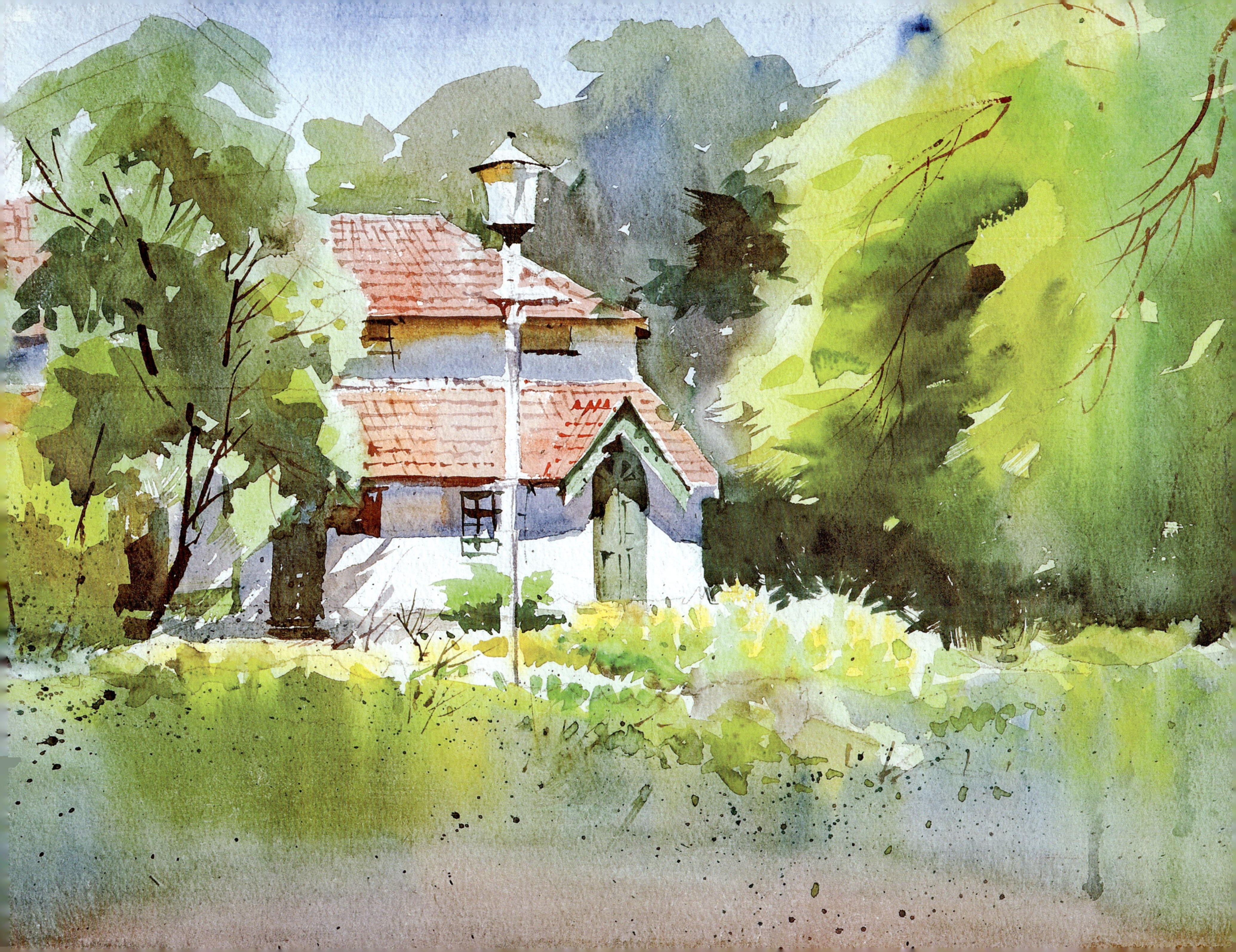

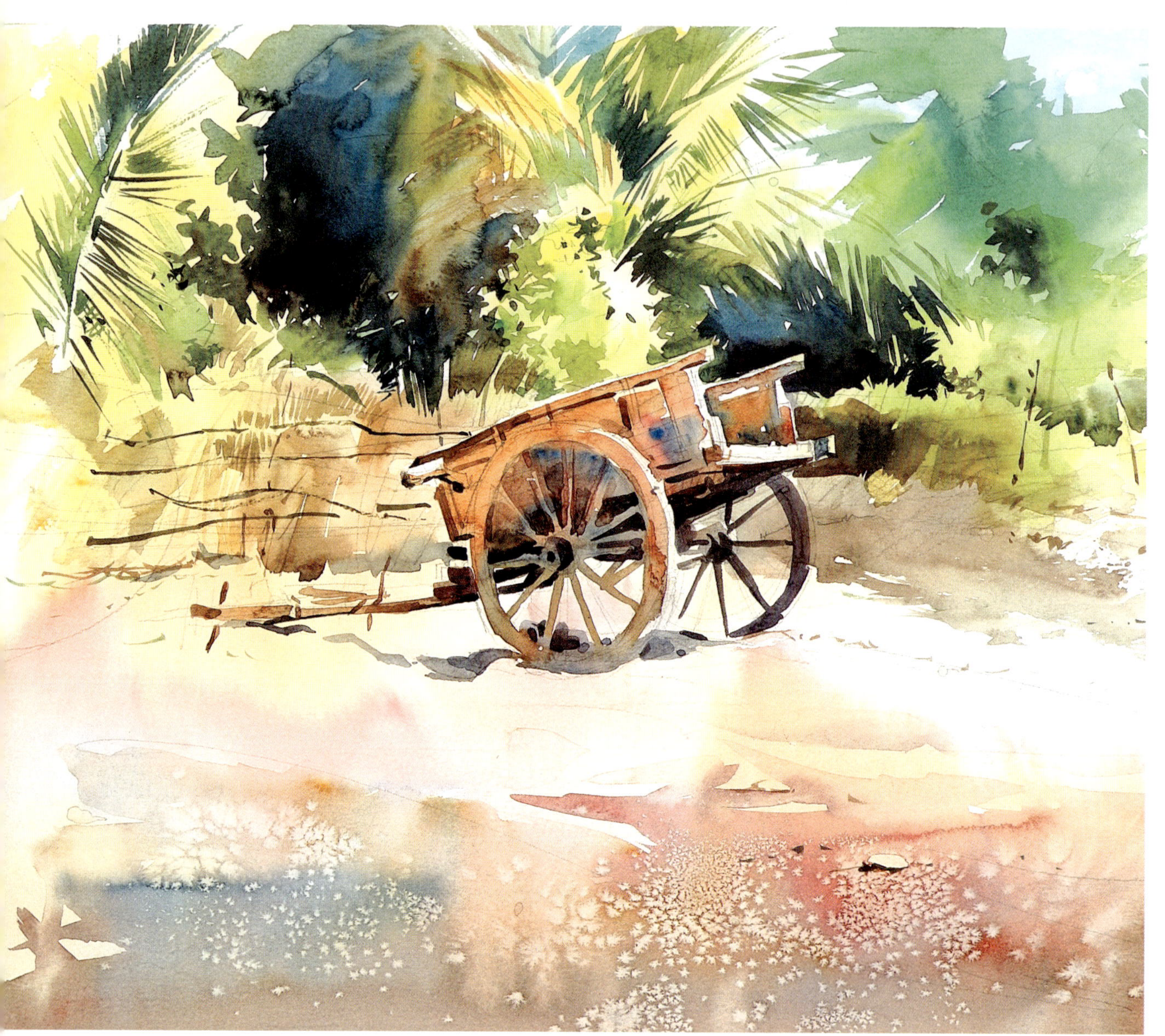

2. Dialogue

One of the important reasons why people find watercolour a daunting medium is because it is difficult to 'control' the paint on paper. We begin by drawing an outline in pencil. Then we wet the paper. Finally when we try to paint within the framework of the pencil drawing, we suddenly find that the paint is behaving independently. We get unplanned masses of colour everywhere. Most of us lose patience at this stage and often give up painting altogether. But take heart – this is actually the fun part of watercolour painting. How to turn this wayward nature of the paint to our advantage is what watercolour painting is all about. Our skill as a painter is to get the shapes we want out of this riot of untamed colours. This process is almost like a dialogue between the artist and his medium. The paints have a mind of their own and the artist has to coax them into working for him.

3. Make mistakes!

Even seasoned artists feel some anxiety every time they are faced with a blank paper. Will I make mistakes? Will the painting turn out to be good? Actually nobody can guarantee that every painting will be like it was conceived in the mind and also be good. This is true of beginners as well as of experienced artists.

In other words, going on painting without looking back at our mistakes is the only way to proceed. You will often find artists repainting the same subject repeatedly. This is to avoid earlier mistakes – and perhaps make new ones! Gaining experience with every mistake is the only way to minimize errors and thereby improve. In a nutshell, this means we have to continue boldly with our playing with colours.

Now, having understood these three 'rules' we are ready to begin....

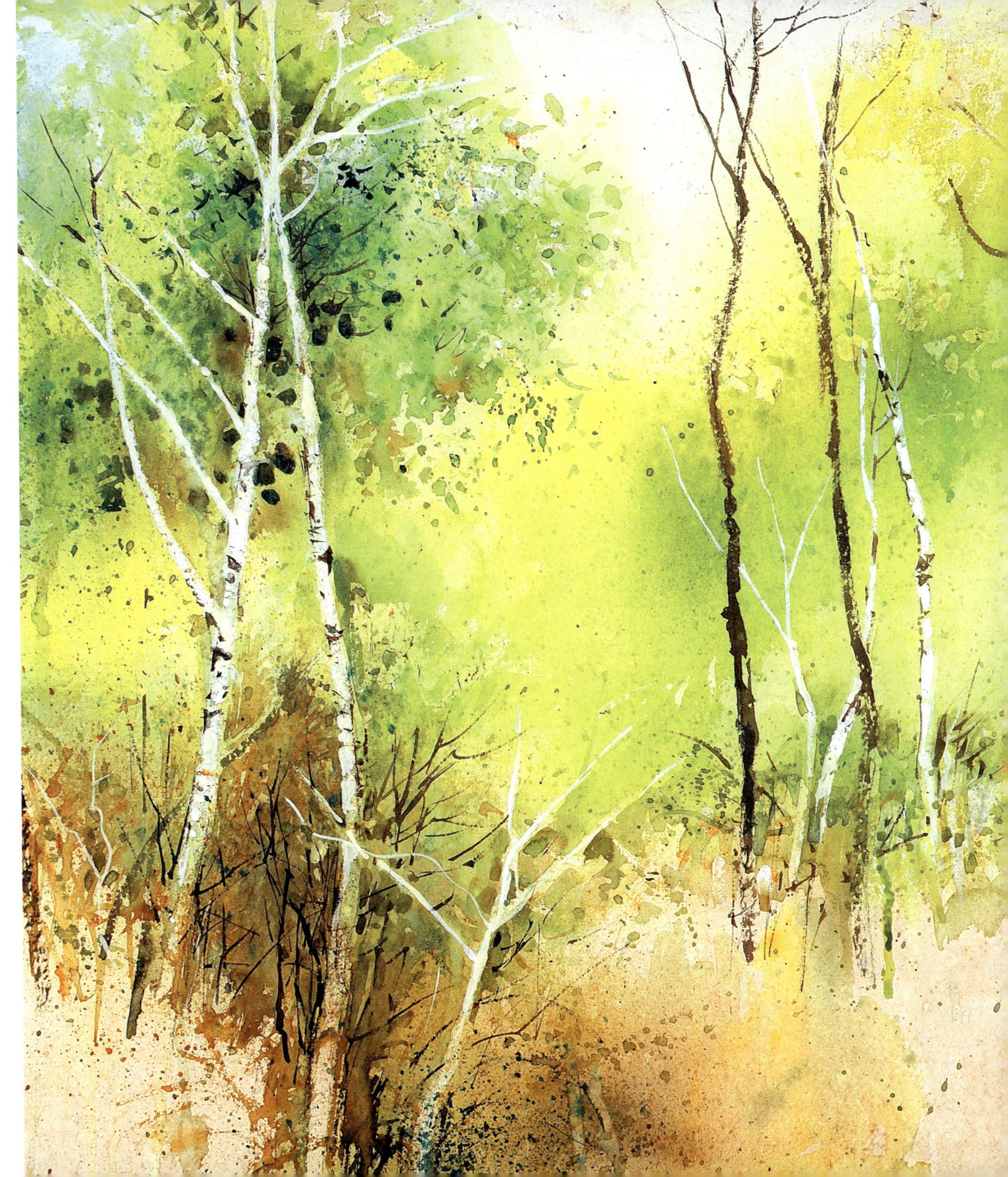

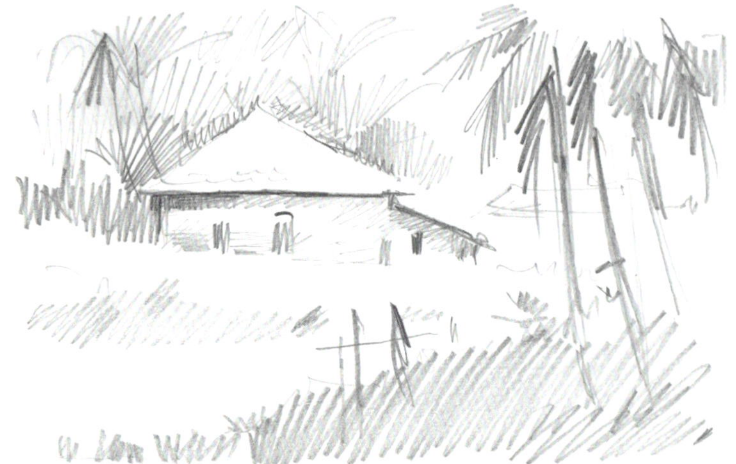

I suggest that you try doing this simple two-step example given alongside, even before you try to understand watercolour techniques.

In the first step I had given a wash with different colours. In the second step I completed the painting using dark shades to depict the shadows, windows and the fronds of the coconut trees.

The thing to remember is the initial wash, which is a very important part of the painting. If you get this wash right, you have completed almost half of your work. After this you can complete the remainder in 2 or 3 steps using one or more techniques that will be described further in the book.

Now let us study the tehniques necessary to learn the further stages of any watercolour painting.

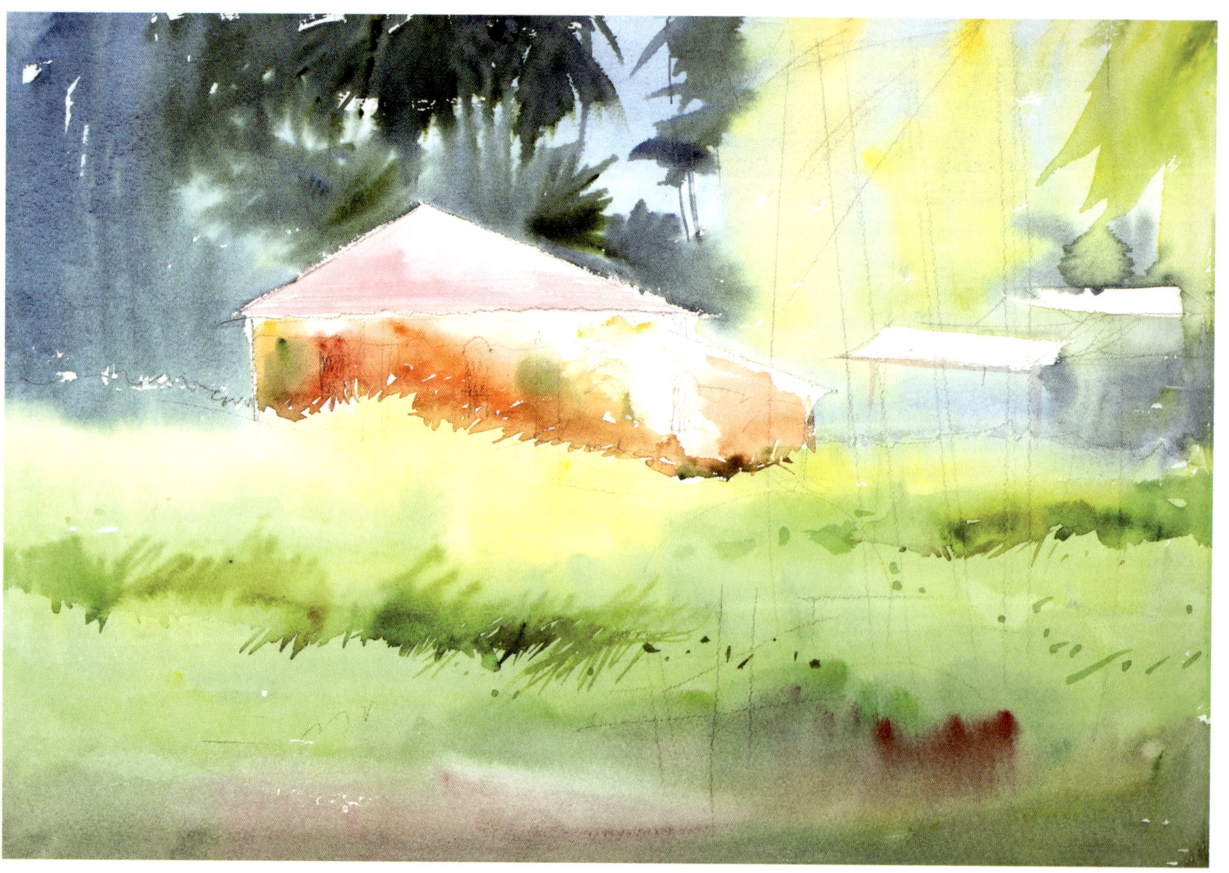

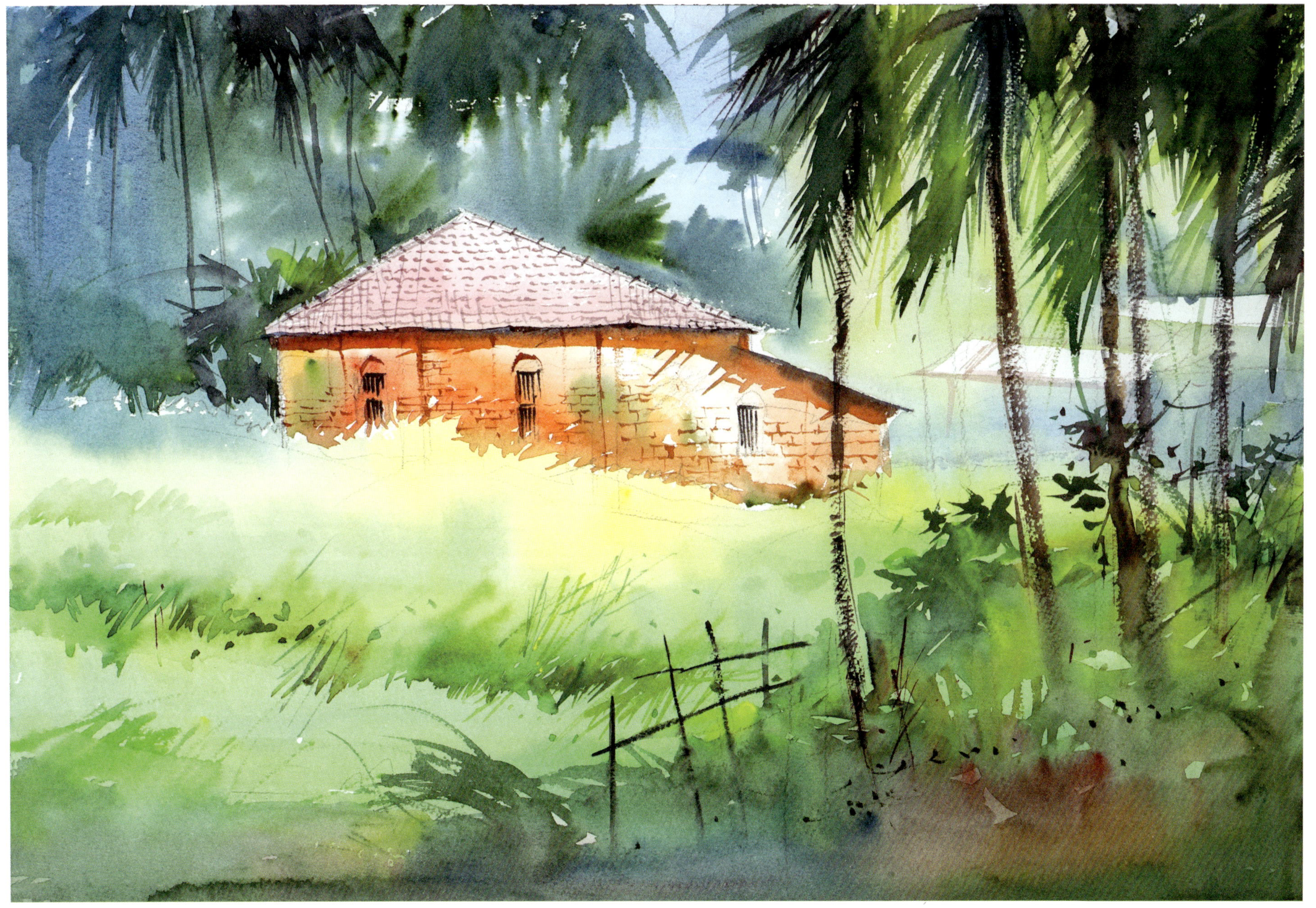

Wash

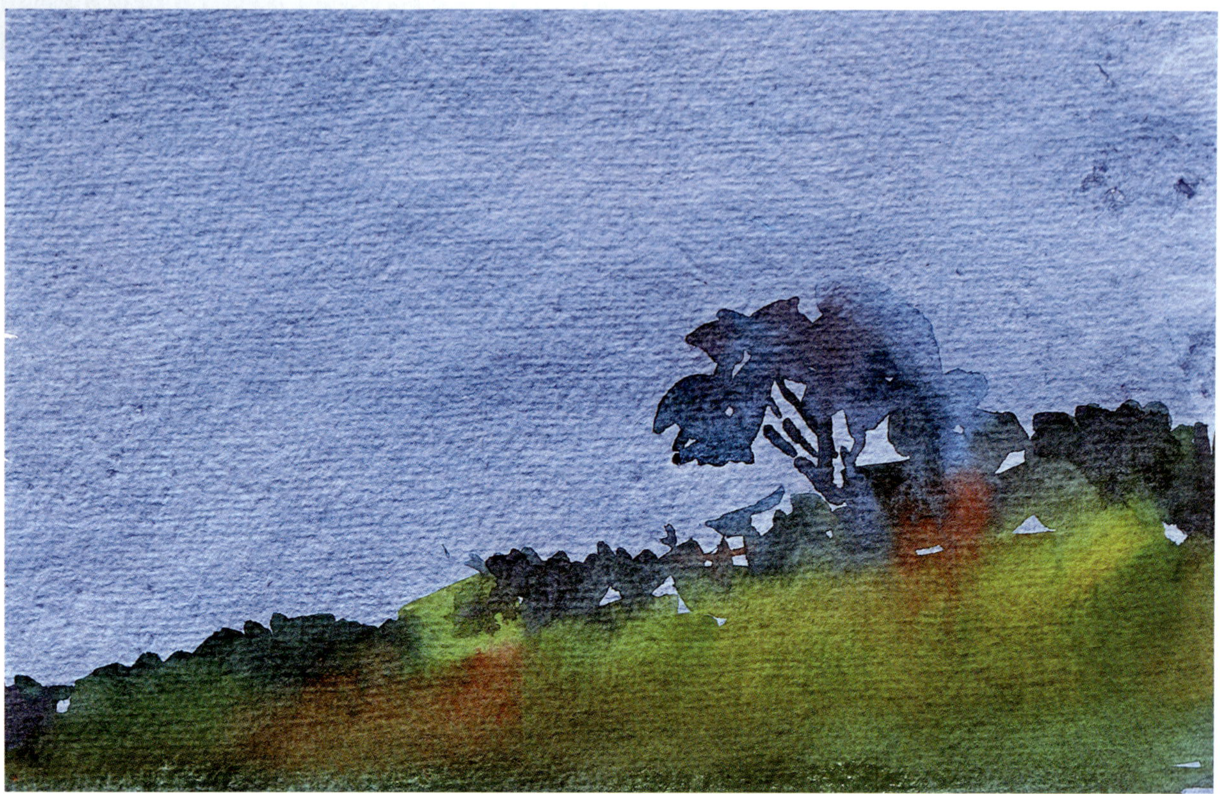

The importance of a wash in any watercolour cannot be overemphasized. Most paintings begin with a wash. It looks deceptively simple but requires a lot of practice to get control over it and achieve a clean and transparent effect. A wash could be plain, graded or variegated.

Plain Wash

Make a thin uniform mixture of any colour in water. Load your brush fully and apply the colour in a left-to-right direction at the upper edge of the paper. Do not 'press' the brush on the paper; just move it lightly over the surface. See that the lower edge of the wash remains wet. Then repeat the process again, taking up the lower edge of the layer just painted and go down successively to the lower edge of the paper. Such a plain wash is used to paint the sky, water or any other large area. If you press the brush too much, the paper surface tends to get damaged or the wash may show bands and patches.

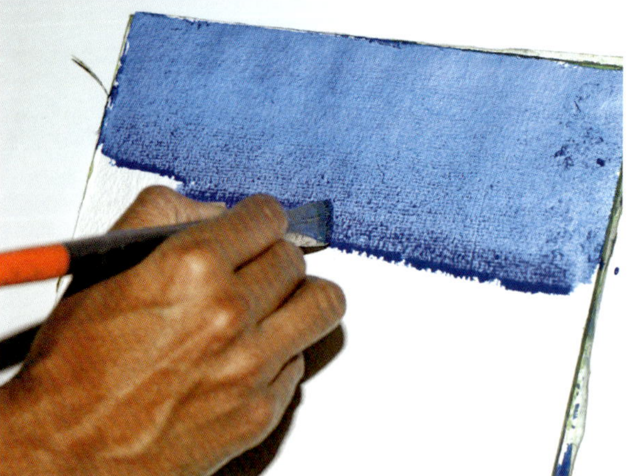

Graded Wash

Here too the direction of the wash is from left to right. The difference from the plain wash is that as you go down, more and more dilute paint is applied (by mixing more and more water). This ensures that the wash gets progressively lighter as you go down to the bottom edge. In fact the last application is almost water with very little paint. Such washes are effective to depict the distant sky.

Now let us use just a few brush strokes on the completely dried wash and see what happens –

A gentle slope and two or three trees have transformed the plain wash into a cloudless sky. (left)

The two hills have suddenly added depth and a feeling of distance to the graded wash. (right)

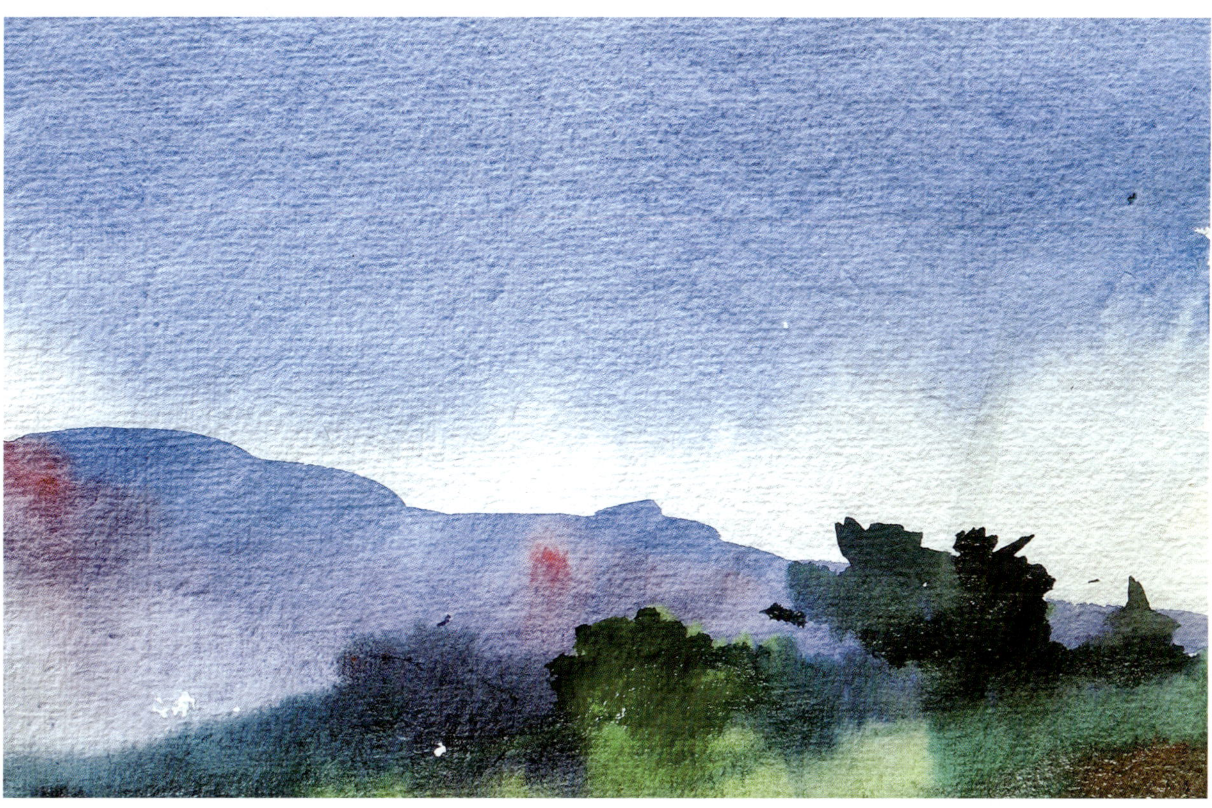

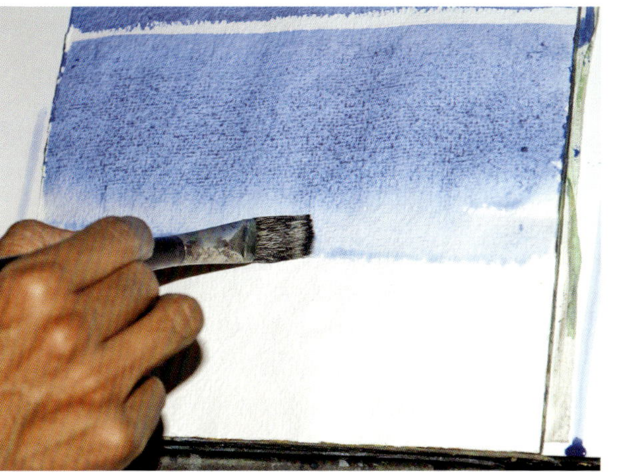

Variegated Wash

Apply a plain wash using any colour. Then, lightly apply a different colour while the first wash is still wet. The wetter the first wash the better the second colour will mix with it. Of course the exact degree of wetness can be achieved only by experience. But once you get the hang of it you can show many beautiful effects.

You must have noticed that we have allowed the paint to flow and mix freely. There is no sharp edge anywhere. Although this sounds simple enough you have to practice these three types of washes quite a lot.

I have shown the distant trees without too many details in the blue-green wash. In the lower part I have added some wash-like strokes in the yellowish-brown. After this, two coconut trees done in blackish blue-green have suddenly made the painting 'complete'. The light blue distant trees and suggestive strokes for the field boundaries have added depth. This was possible only because of the variegated wash.

Assignment One

Practice giving washes of different sizes and using different colours as described here. I would especially recommend using at least three colours to practice a variegated wash.

Here, I have moved the brush horizontally while applying paint. You may also try making vertical and oblique strokes.

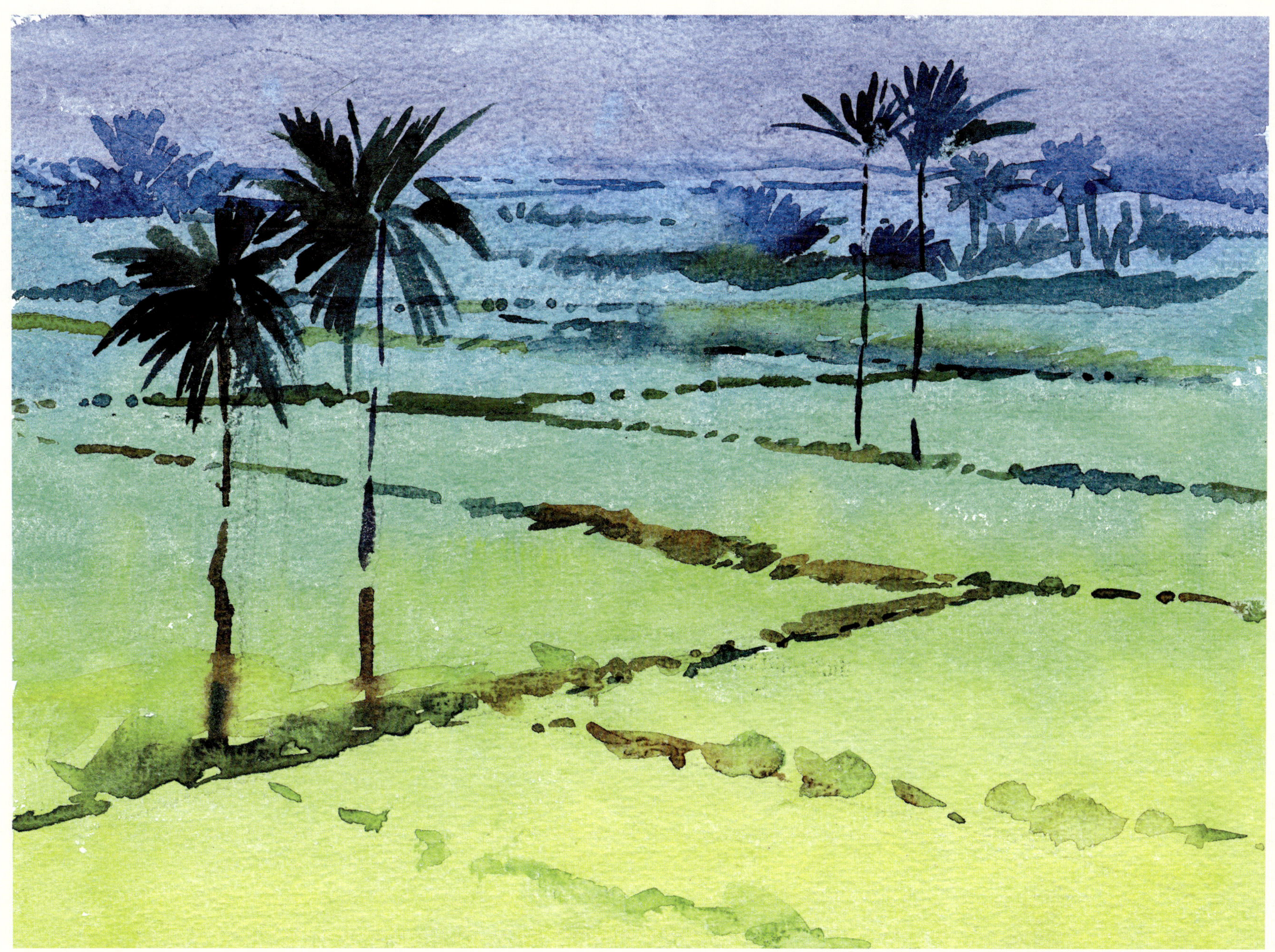

Lesson Two

Wet-in-Wet 1

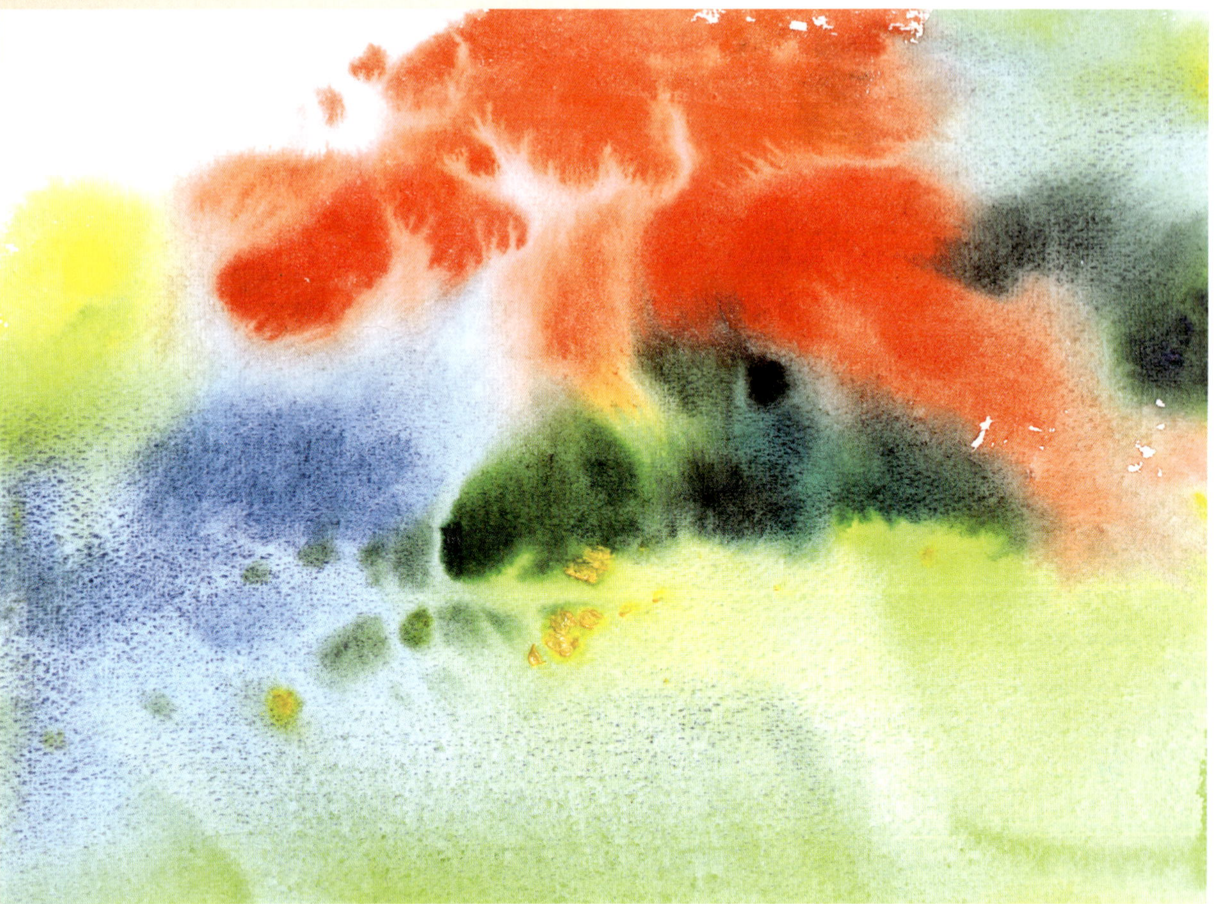

These are the beautiful effects we get when the wet colours are allowed to mix freely with each other on a completely wet paper surface. Here, I dipped a sheet of paper in a bucket of water. But even before that my palette was kept in readiness. I had mixed all the required colours in abundant quantity.

Now if you are ready, take up a colour in your brush and lightly 'drop' it onto the wet paper. Do not 'apply' the paint by using undue pressure on the brush. Then apply the second colour into the first colour while it is still wet. You will see that the two colours blend imperceptibly into one another. Now hold two diagonally opposite corners of the paper and move it gently in all directions and see how interesting effects are created.

Next, let us see what we can do with this wash which has dried. You would have realized that by applying two or three dark patches below the red wash, we suddenly have a gulmohor tree against the blue-green background which suggests dense foliage.

When we paint outdoors we see a variety of trees with different colours, shapes, leaves and branches. It is both impossible and unnecessary to paint in every detail. We can achieve the overall effect by using the wet-in-wet technique. It goes without saying that lots of practice is necessary before you gain reasonable control over the medium.

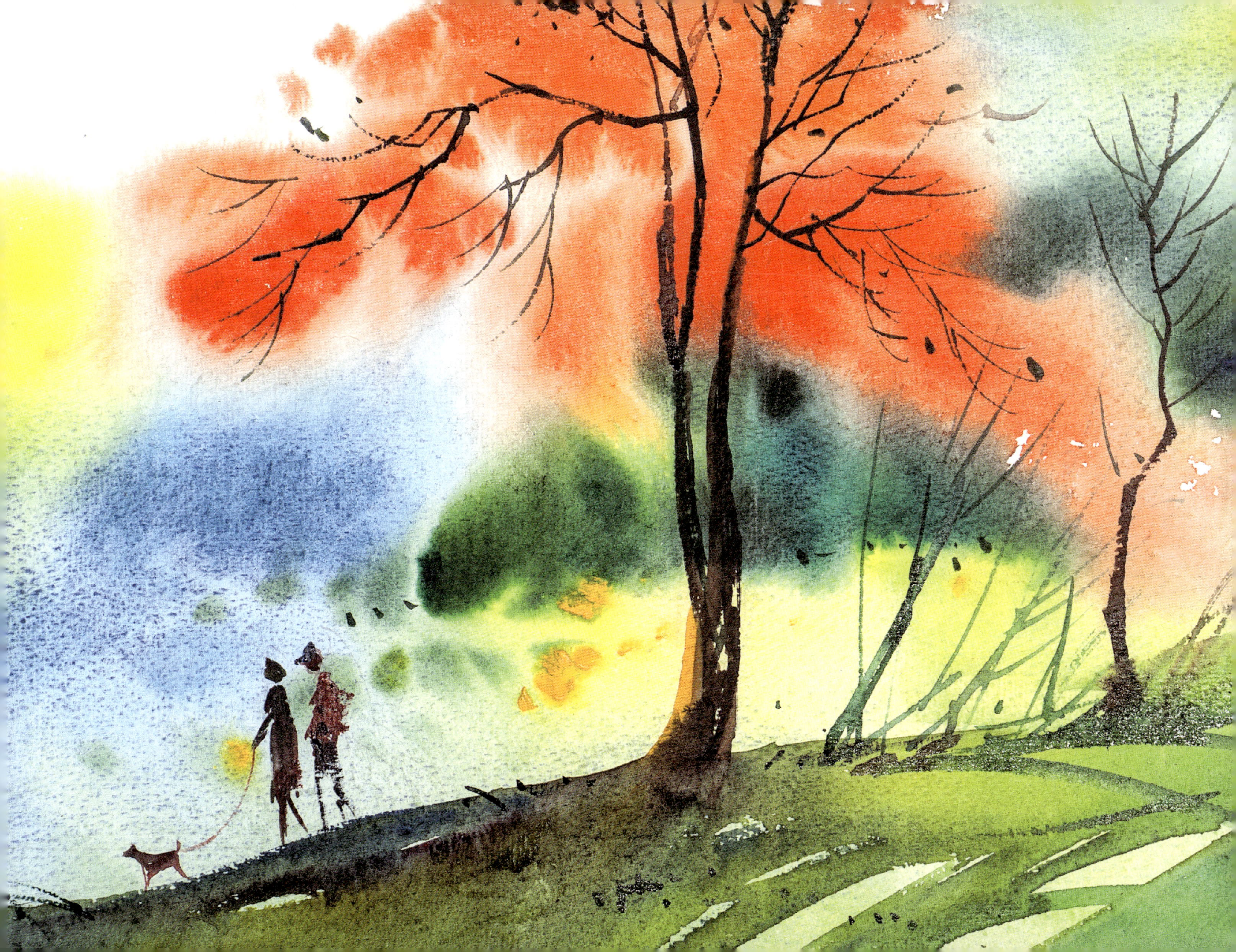

Before we go on to learn other techniques, let us look a bit at the wetness of the paper on which we paint and the thickness (consistency) of the paint we apply. When we paint the paper may be absolutely dry, or totally wet or in some intermediate stage of wetness. Depending on how wet the paper is, there is a simple logic as to how thick the paint should be in order to get the desired effect. So, what are the stages of wetness?

1. Wet – This when the paper can be said to be 'glistening' wet.

2. Damp – This stage occurs about 3-4 minutes after the first stage.

3. Moist – This is about 3-4 minutes after the damp paper has been kept untouched.

4. Dry – Here, there is no trace of moisture at all.

Now, in order to understand the varying thickness of paint that can be used, let us consider this analogy. The most dilute paint can be likened to 'tea'. A little thicker paint can be like 'coffee'. Somewhat thicker than that is like 'milk'. If you use even lesser water to mix up paint it becomes as thick as cream. Finally, if almost undiluted paint directly from the tube is used, it is as thick as butter. Note that we are *not* considering the *colour* of tea or coffee etc; nor are we considering 'milk' as a whitener to lighten the paints. We have used the analogy to understand increasing 'thickness' of paints as we are going to use them.

To put it differently I have given a table that shows the ratio of paint to water.

Let us understand this further with the help of the 5 patches of blue given alongside –

1. When applied 'out of the tube' with very little water – this dark blue that we get is like butter in consistency.

2. With 30% water added, the blue is of cream-like consistency and is lighter in shade than the above.

3. The bright blue here is a result of mixing half paint and half water.

4. Add more water (70%) and we get the consistency of coffee.

5. With almost no paint – 90% water, we get a very thin, tea-like consistency and the result is a very light blue.

Now our job is to try and study how each of these five consistencies of colour behaves, on each of the four stages of wetness of the paper. This is one exercise that will come in handy at every step on our journey as a watercolour painter. For this we need to know how colours behave on paper in different stages of wetness.

Water		Colour	Dencity
10%	+	90%	Butter
30%	+	70%	Cream
50%	+	50%	Milk
70%	+	30%	Coffee
90%	+	10%	Tea

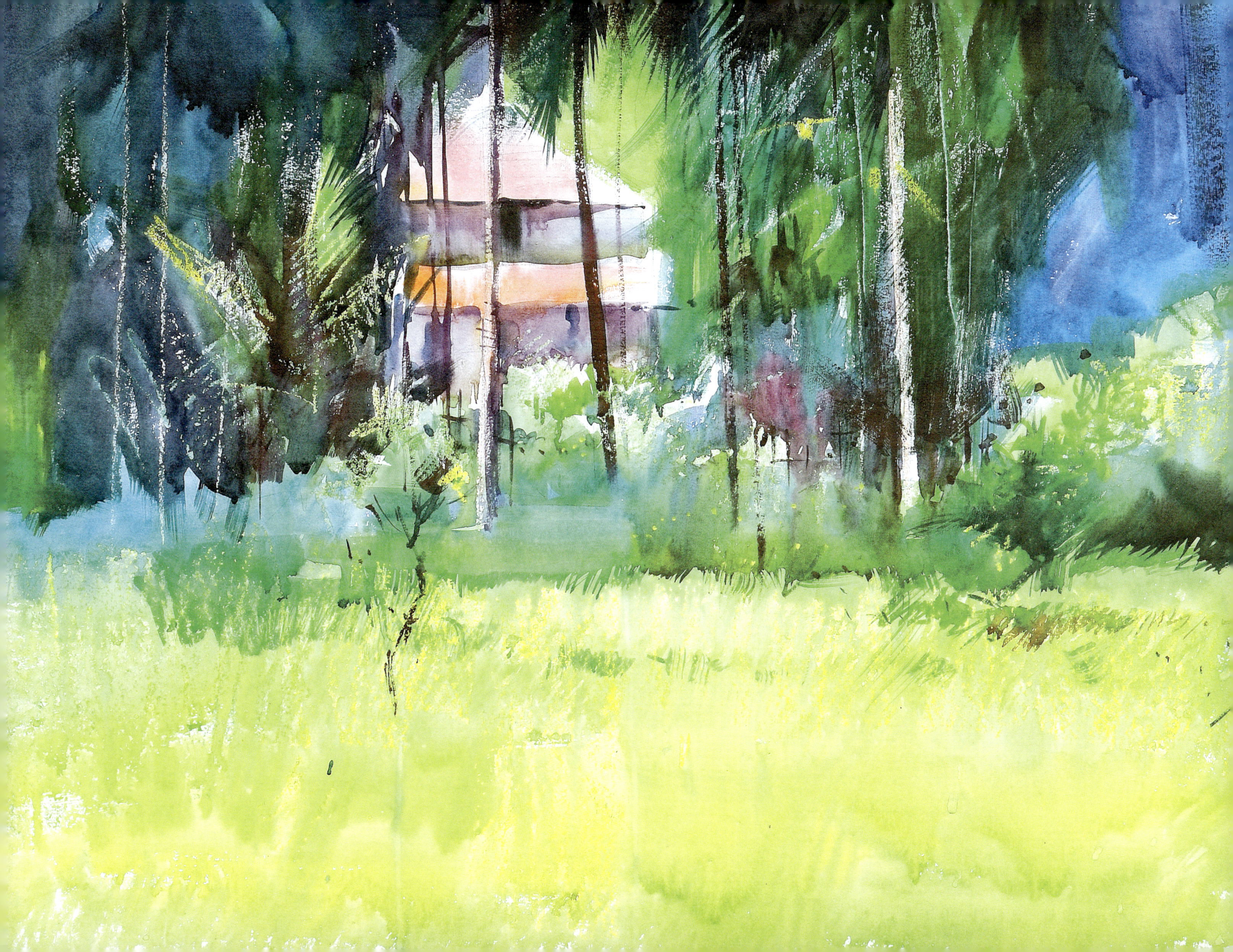

Now we are going to see how colours flow on 'damp' and 'moist' paper. Similarly we are going to see how the thickness of colour correlates with the different stages of wetness of the paper.

Take a paper and dip it completely in water so that it is wet. Before that keep your palette ready with colours of different consistency in the manner of our 'tea-coffee' analogy. Now apply these different thicknesses of paint on this wet paper and observe how they intermix.

Now dip another paper as before but wait for 3-4 minutes. The paper will be 'damp'. Go over the previous exercise of applying the paint in the five stages of thickness.

Take another paper and apply water all over it with a large brush. The paper will not be uniformly wet as it did earlier. Apply paint again and observe. Slowly you will get the hang of it.

Sometimes while indulging in this play of colours we find peculiar patches developing on the paper – these are called ‘cauliflowers’. They occur as ‘accidents’ and are generally unwelcome. Also there is no fool-proof way to avoid them, except by experience. These cauliflowers are more likely to happen if the paint is too dilute or ‘thin’ (tea, coffee or milk!) while applying onto a semi-wet (damp / moist) paper. Thicker paint (cream or butter) minimizes the possibility.

Since there is no way we can measure the wetness of paper, we can learn the exact thickness of paint to be used and the paper's wetness only by experience.

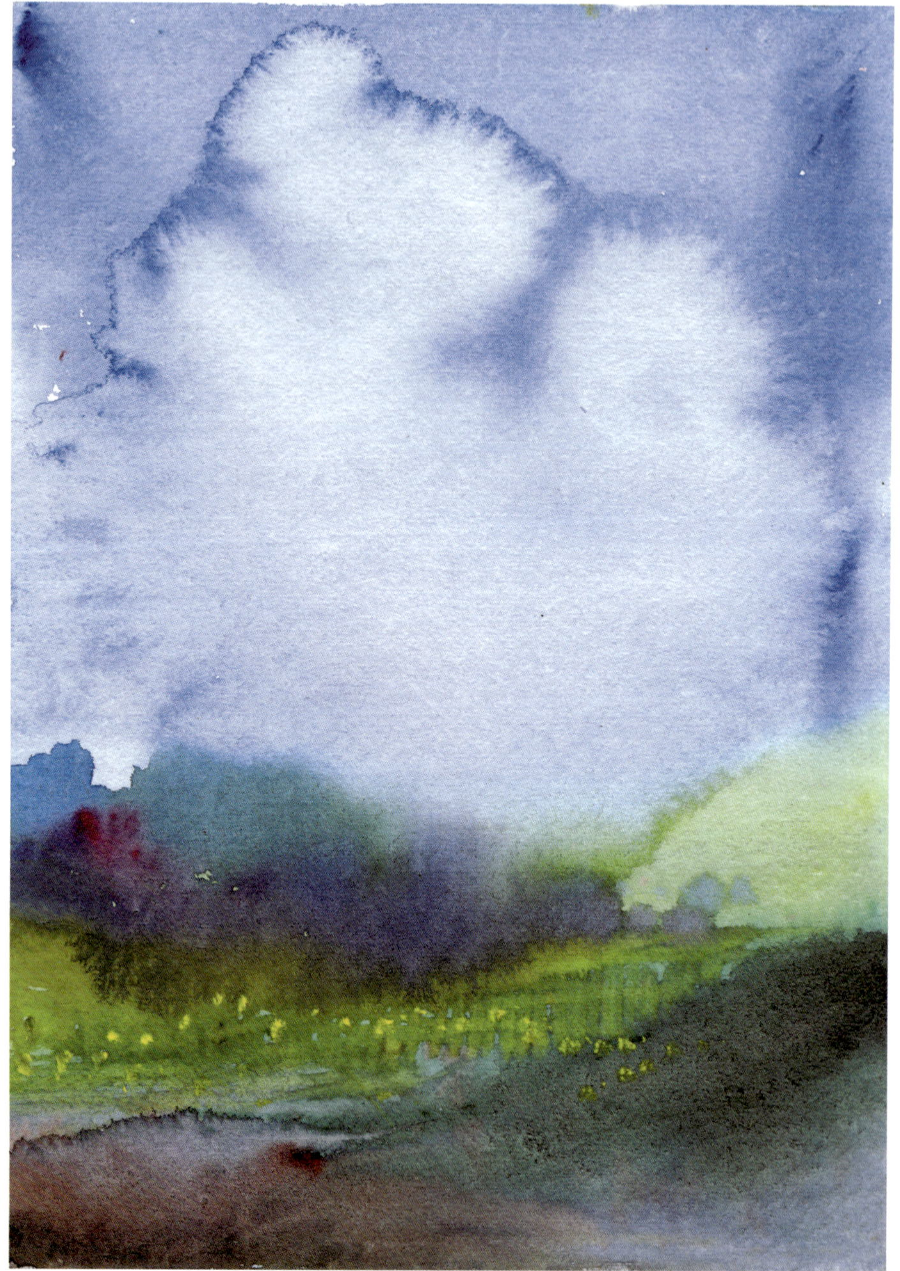

Assignment Two

Experiment freely with the wet-in-wet effect. Do this with some image in mind or even with no specific object. Change the shades and colours. Then, as a further step, try creating a picture from the shapes you get.

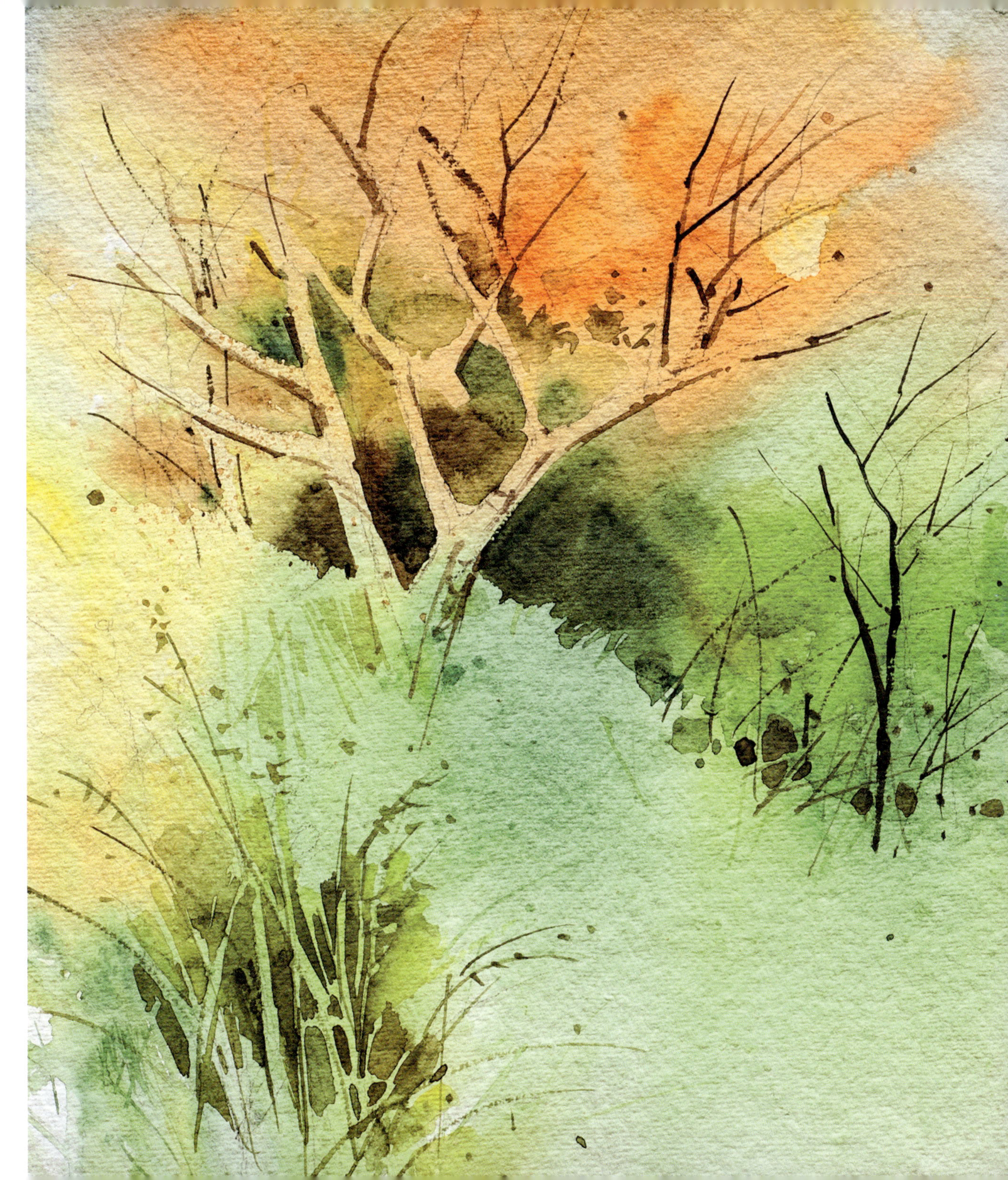

On rare occasions such as in this painting, cauliflowers can be used effectively – as they have been made into clouds here.

Lesson Three

Wet-in-Wet 2

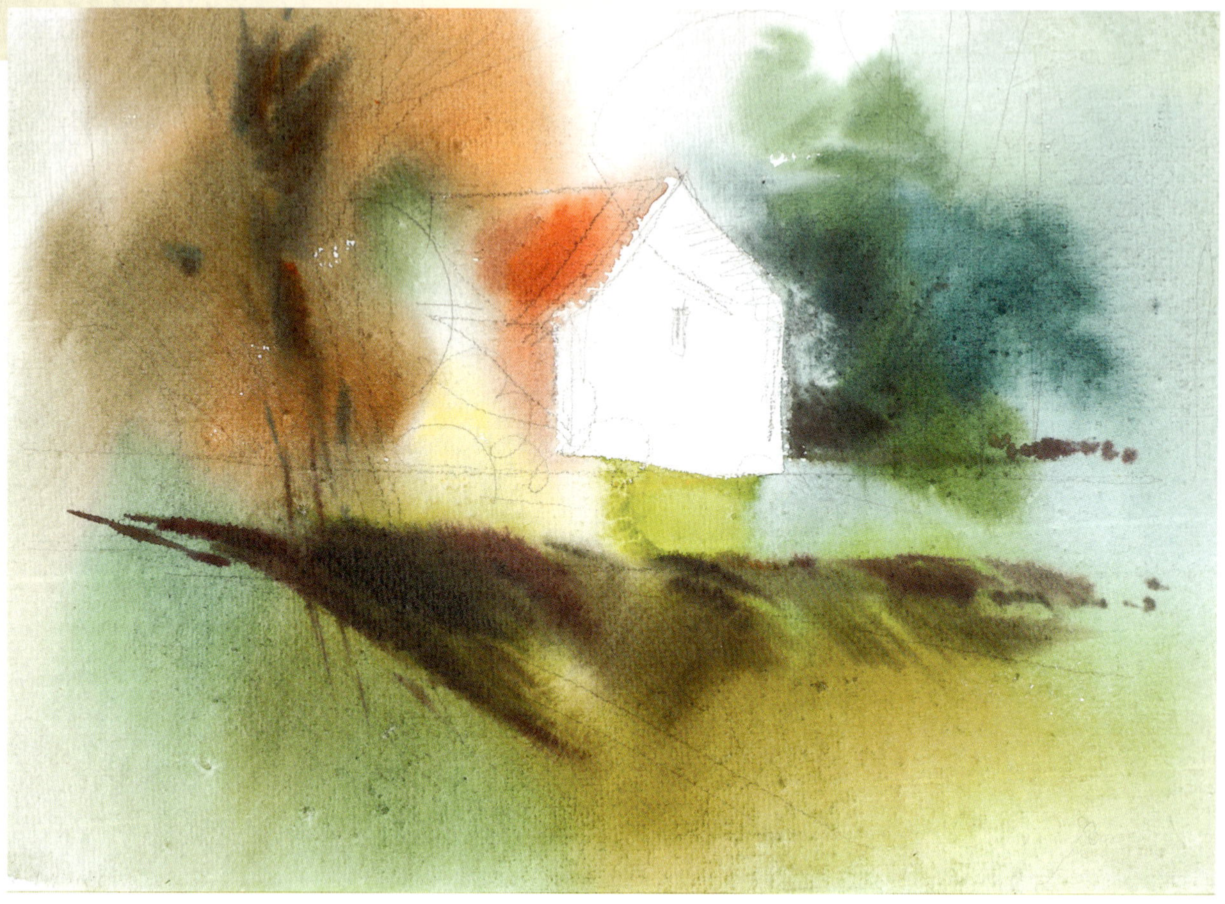

Wet-in-wet in a controlled area

In the adjoining painting we are going to leave the wall and roof unpainted while achieving the wet-in-wet effect in the remaining parts.

With the minimum of lines I have penciled in the outline of the house and the adjoining road and slope. With a flat brush I applied water all over the paper leaving the house untouched. Immediately thereafter I applied different colours wet-in-wet. There was a definite thought behind this. I considered the background foliage, road and the slope etc. Some of the colours are thin (tea), some are thicker (cream), and yet others are less thick (coffee / milk). The thin colours flow freely on the paper while the thicker ones flow less easily; if the paint is thick, only the edges get mixed easily.

After the paint has dried you will realize that all the desired effects have been achieved by just one wet-in-wet wash. By choosing the colours carefully and how they are applied, half the battle is won.

In step 2 I have used a reddish colour for the roof and purple for its shadow. Suddenly the house seems to be bathed in bright sunlight. All that remained to be done now was the two tree trunks and some dark patches on the slope.

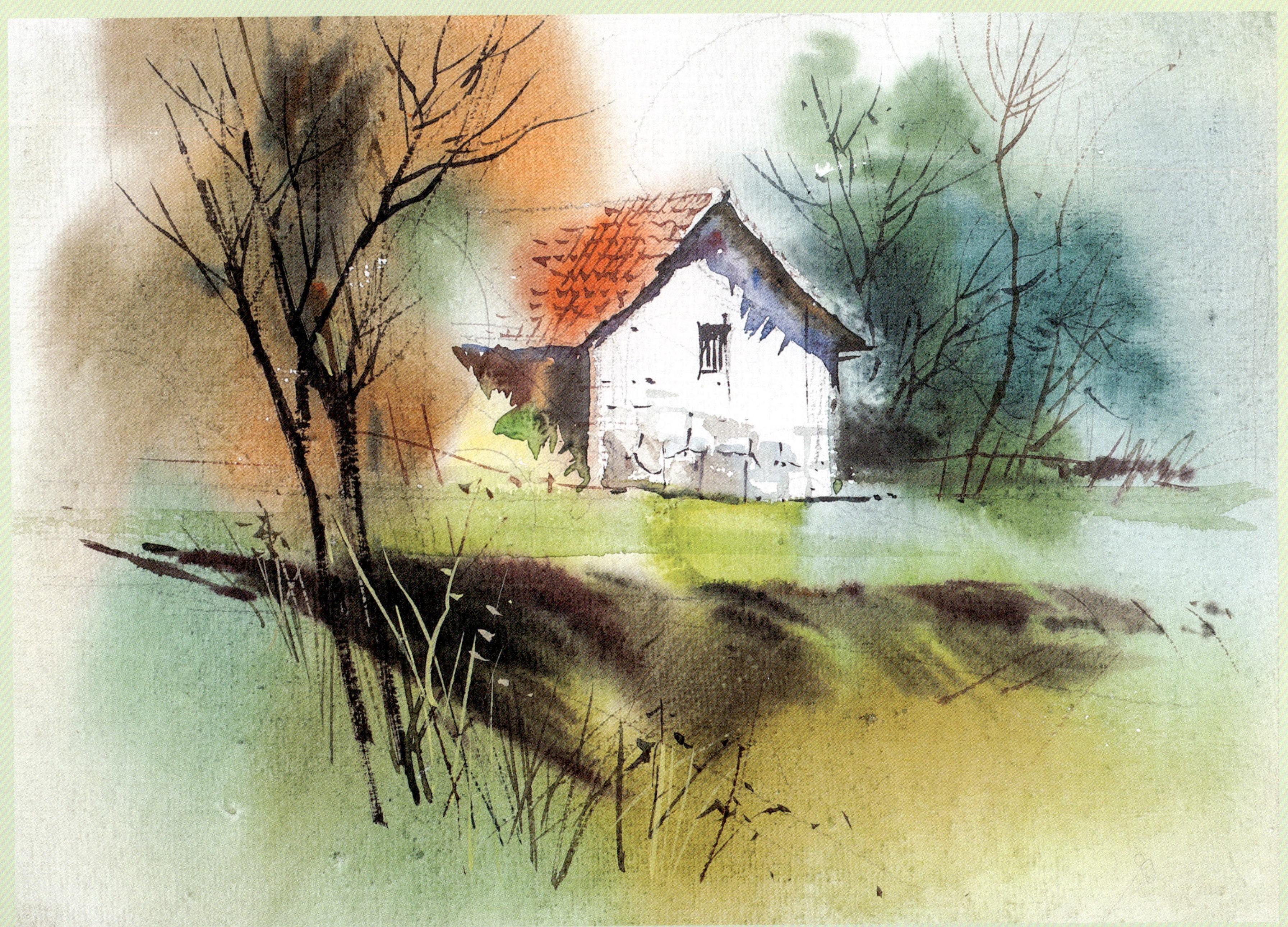

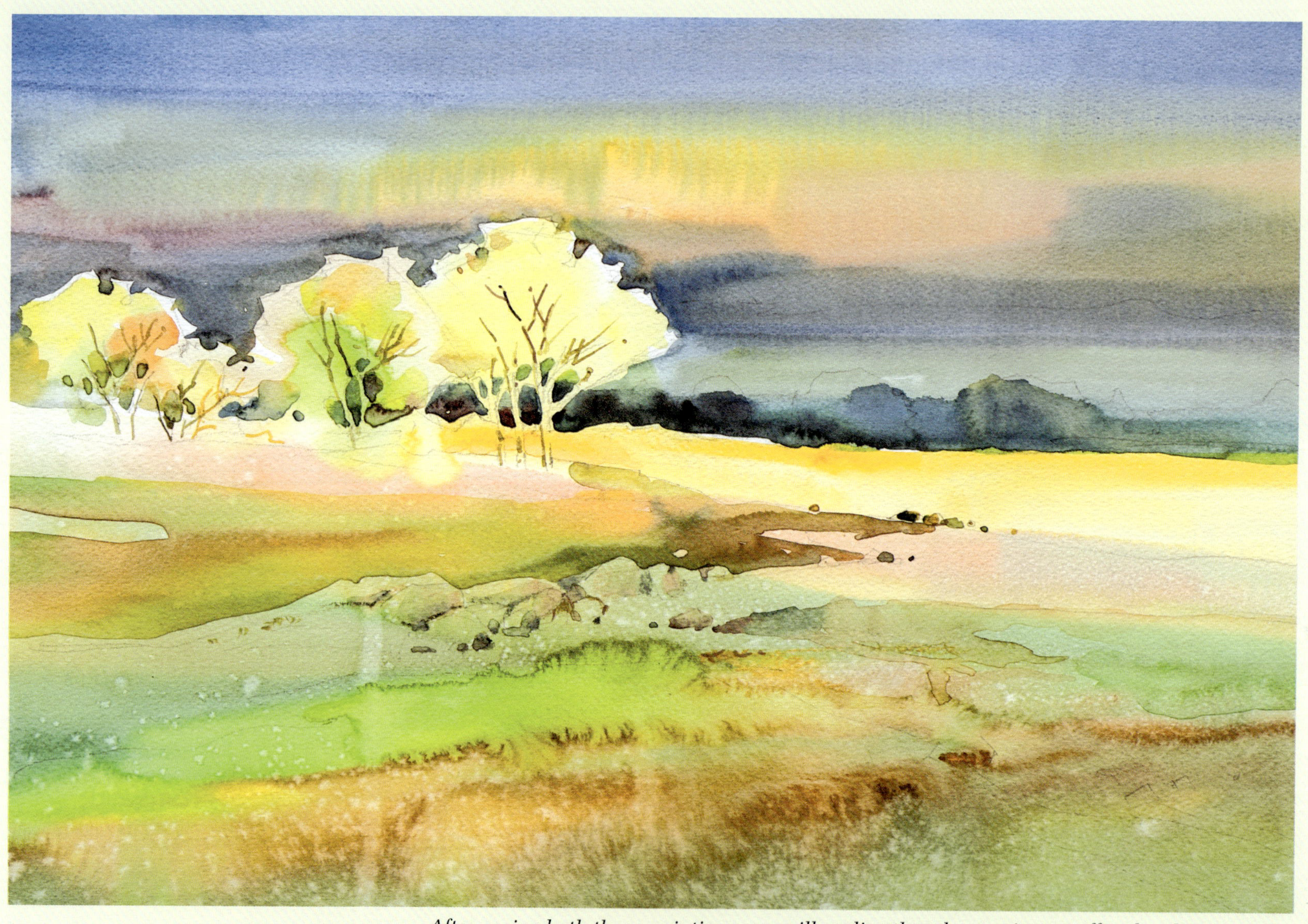

After seeing both these paintings you will realize that the wet-in-wet effect has been used in certain parts only; elsewhere, I have allowed the sharp edges to remain. We can get our forms perfectly if we gain control over this selective use of the wet-in-wet technique.

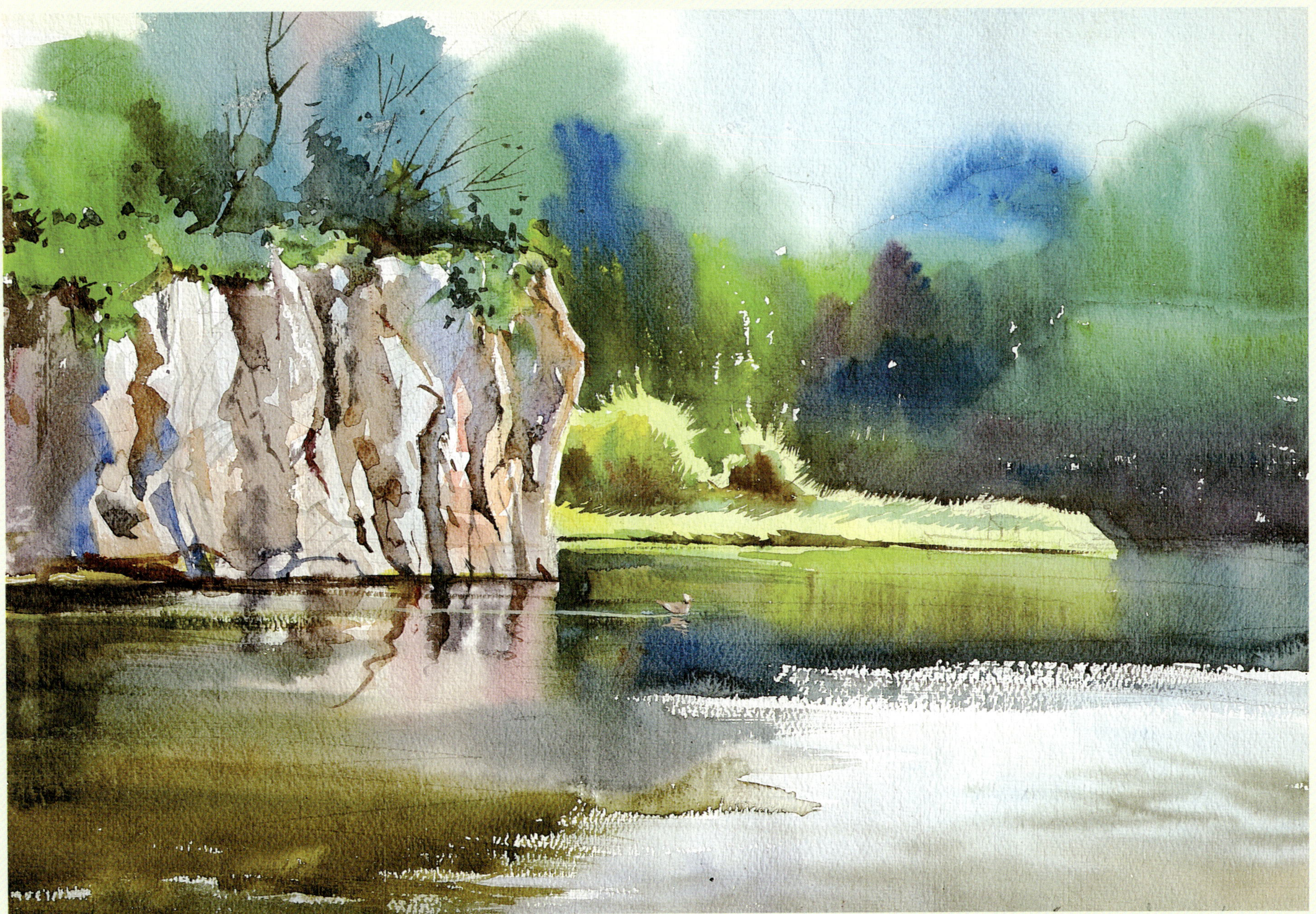

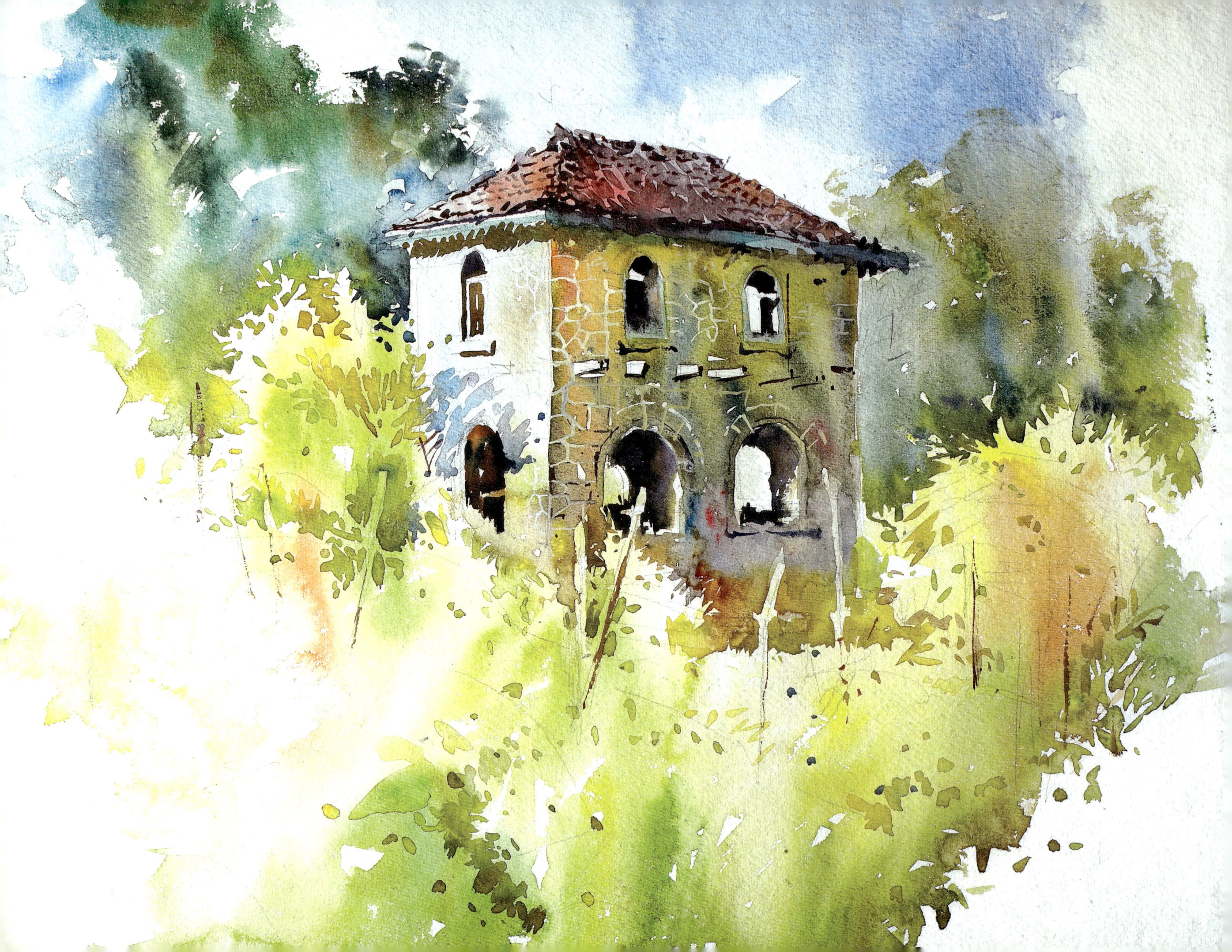

Assignment Three

Now wet a part of the paper and use the wet-in-wet method on the area. Then begin your own experiments. Keep unpainted spaces for the boats or the bougainvillea flowers and try out the wet-in-wet technique in the other areas of the painting.

The background foliage in green and the yellow foreground bushes have been done wet-in-wet. Some sharp edges have been allowed to develop. Even the shadow portion of the house is a mass of wet-in-wet.

In this painting there is only a free riot of colours and some sharp edges. There are no trees, houses, bullock-carts or any objects. But see how a painting can be made with pure colour only.

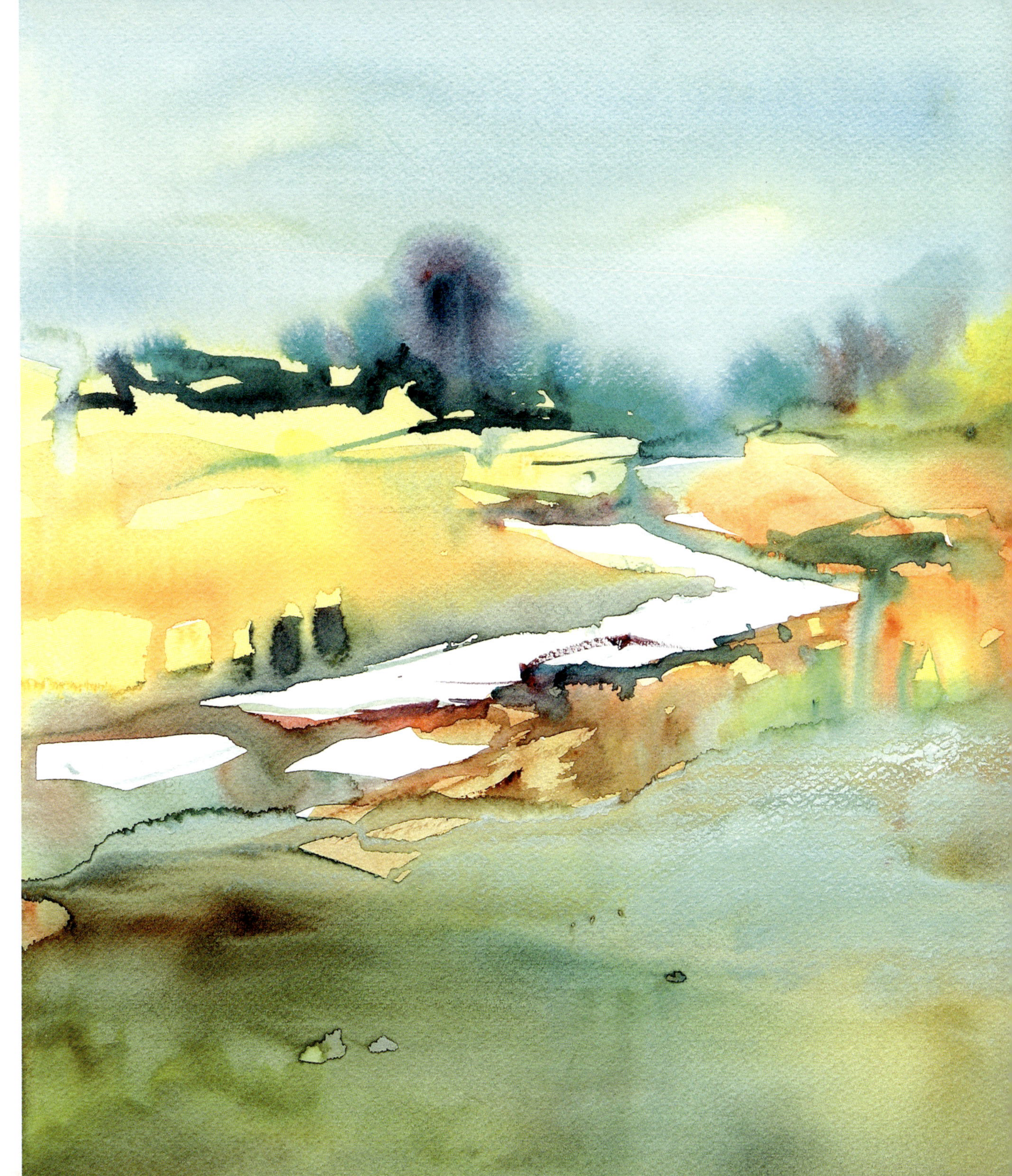

About the colour wheel

We know that red, blue and yellow are the primary colours. By mixing these, we get the secondary colours viz. violet, green and orange. Theoretically if we mix the three primaries together we should get black, but in reality we get blackish grey. Even if we mix red and green (instead of blue and yellow) we get this blackish grey. So also if we mix any primary colour with a secondary colour got by mixing the other two primary ones, we get this blackish grey.

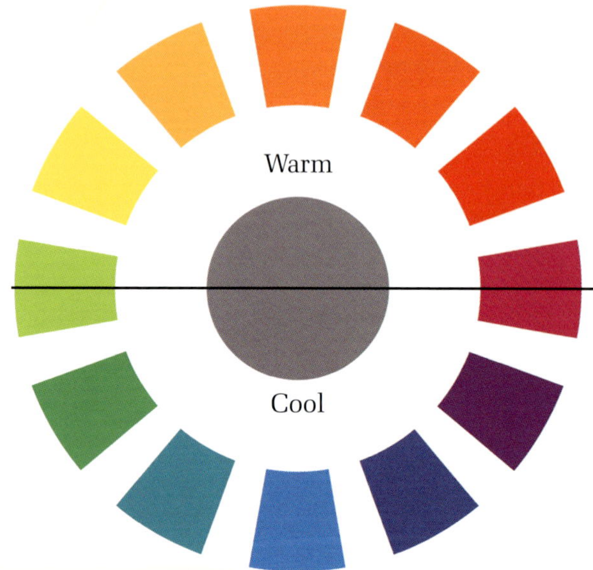

In the colour wheel, the colour opposite any colour is called the complementary colour.

The figure alongside has two pairs of colours. The first pair is vermilion red and sap green. This is the pair of 'warm' colours.The other pair of crimson red and viridian green is the 'cool' pair. When these two are mixed we get a warm brown or cool brown (with a violet tinge) respectively.

Depending on the requirement of a painting, we can use the correct complementary colours to get the desired dark shades.

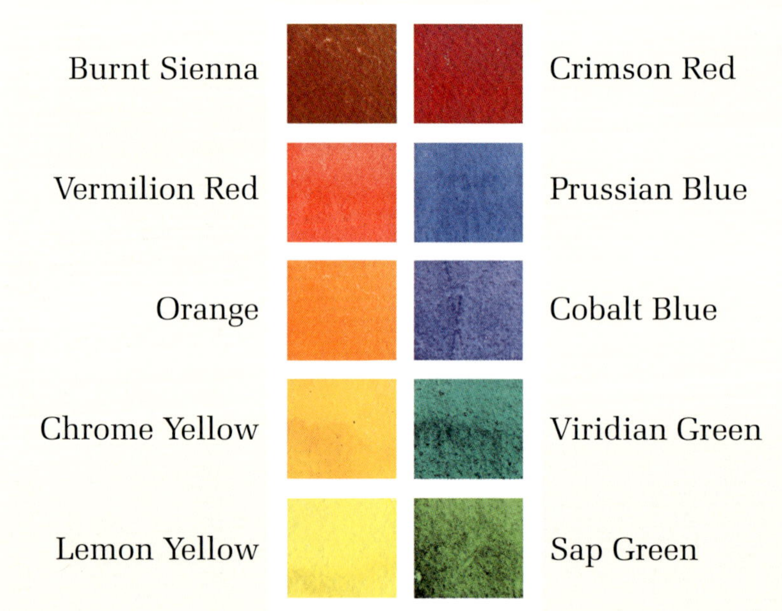

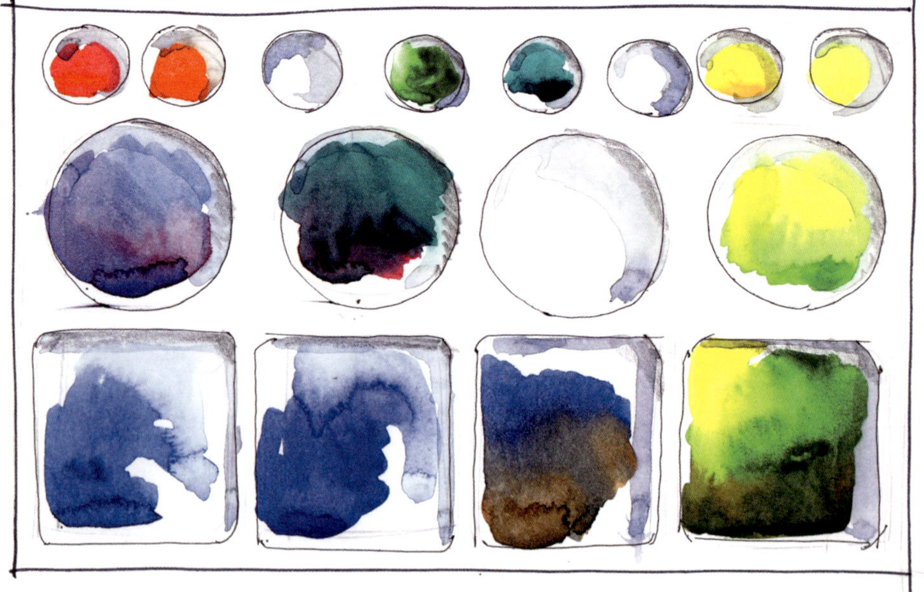

When we set out our palette we must keep the colour wheel in mind. Usually I prepare the paints in my palette as shown in the accompanying figure. This keeps the colour wheel ready in front of my eyes and makes it easy to mix the desired shades.

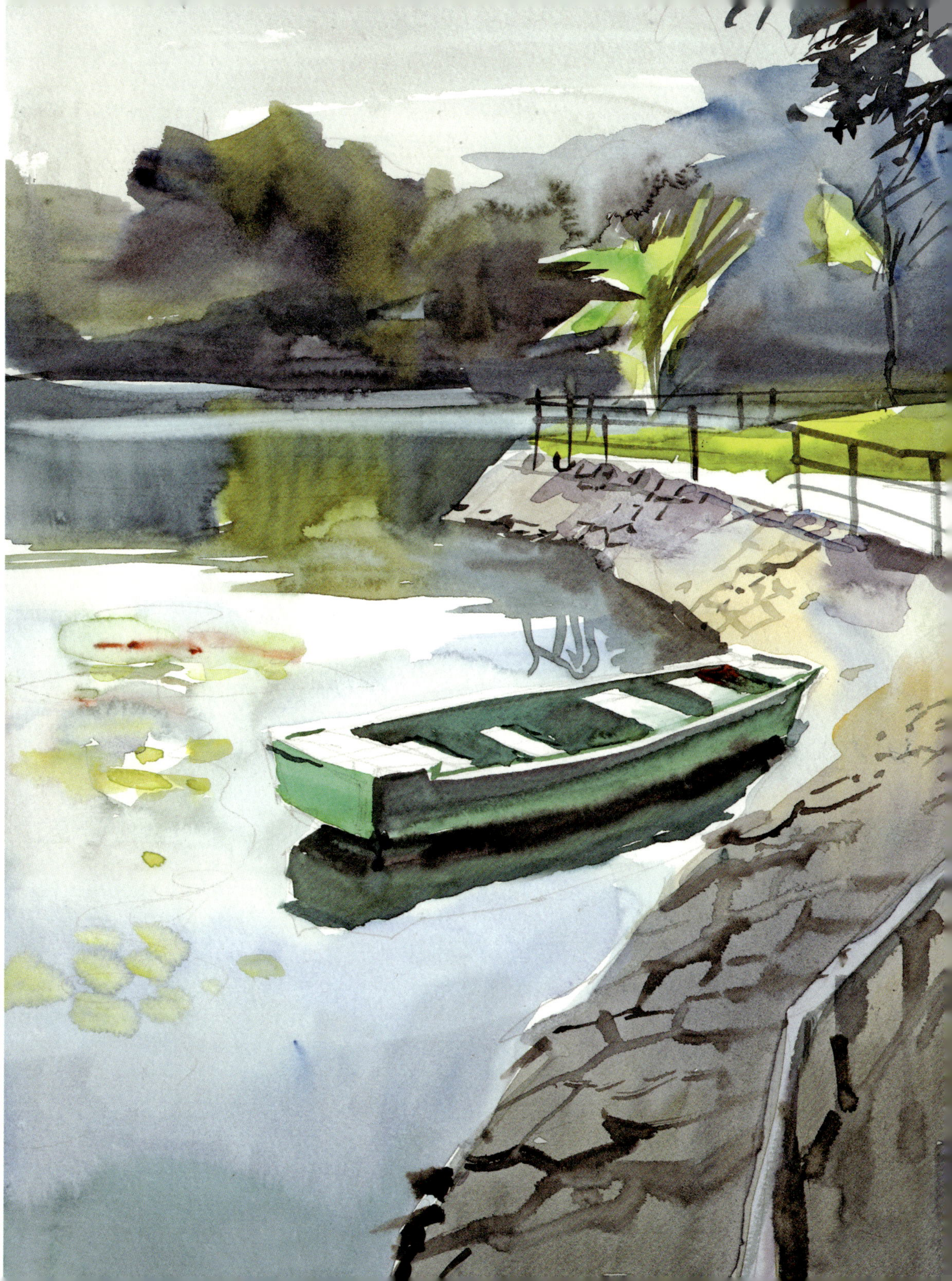

Glazing

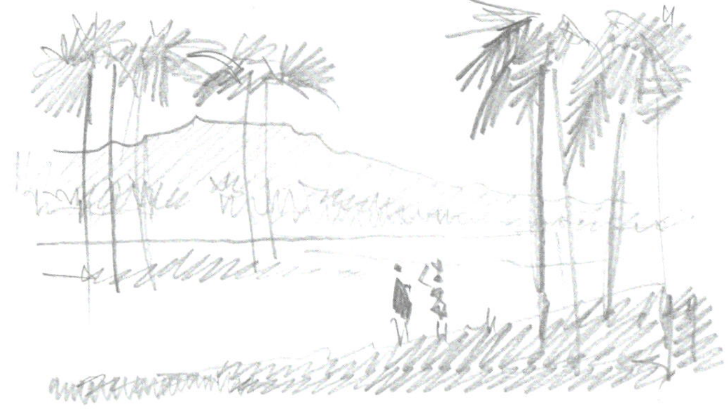

To put it simply, glazing means the application of one or more washes upon another which has dried completely. More than three washes can thus be applied, though the brush needs to be moved lightly over the paper so as not to damage the surface or spoil the underlying wash.

We know that transparency is the hallmark of a good watercolour. The underlying paper is 'seen' through a wash. Similarly the first wash is partly seen through the second wash that is applied over it. The result is a third, different tone. This is not the same tone as you will get if the two concerned colours are mixed in a palette and then applied.

It is worth remembering that most of us use hand-made paper of Indian make. The limitation of this paper is that we can apply a maximum of 5-6 washes one over the other on this paper. Beyond that the surface gets damaged. Also, the more the washes, the more chances there are of losing transparency. There are some artists who are said to have applied almost 100 washes on very high quality imported paper.

Let us now do a painting using the technique of glazing.

Step 1 depicts a typical coastal Konkan scene with the basic elements sketched lightly in pencil. Green fields stretch into the distance, beyond which there is a bluish-looking mountain. The foreground has a few coconut trees.

First I applied a variegated wash from top to bottom using lemon yellow and green. I mixed some red at the bottom.

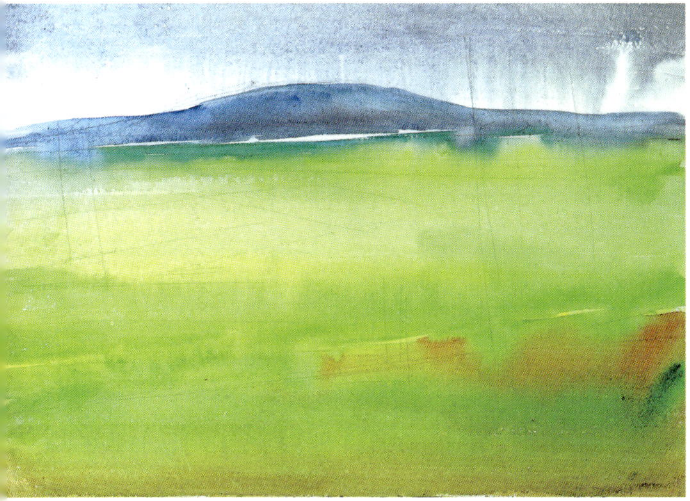

When this was completely dry, I painted the mountain in cobalt blue ('coffee' consistency) with a dash of brown in some places.

This blue-brown, along with the underlying blue wash has given a unique blueness to the mountain. In places where there was a yellow-green wash, I have added a blue-green wash in some areas. The yellow-green-blue layers on top of each other have given a bright sheen to the fields. When the second wash had dried I used the same blue but slightly thicker (milk), to depict the distant trees. At the same time I painted the embankments in the lower portion of the painting.

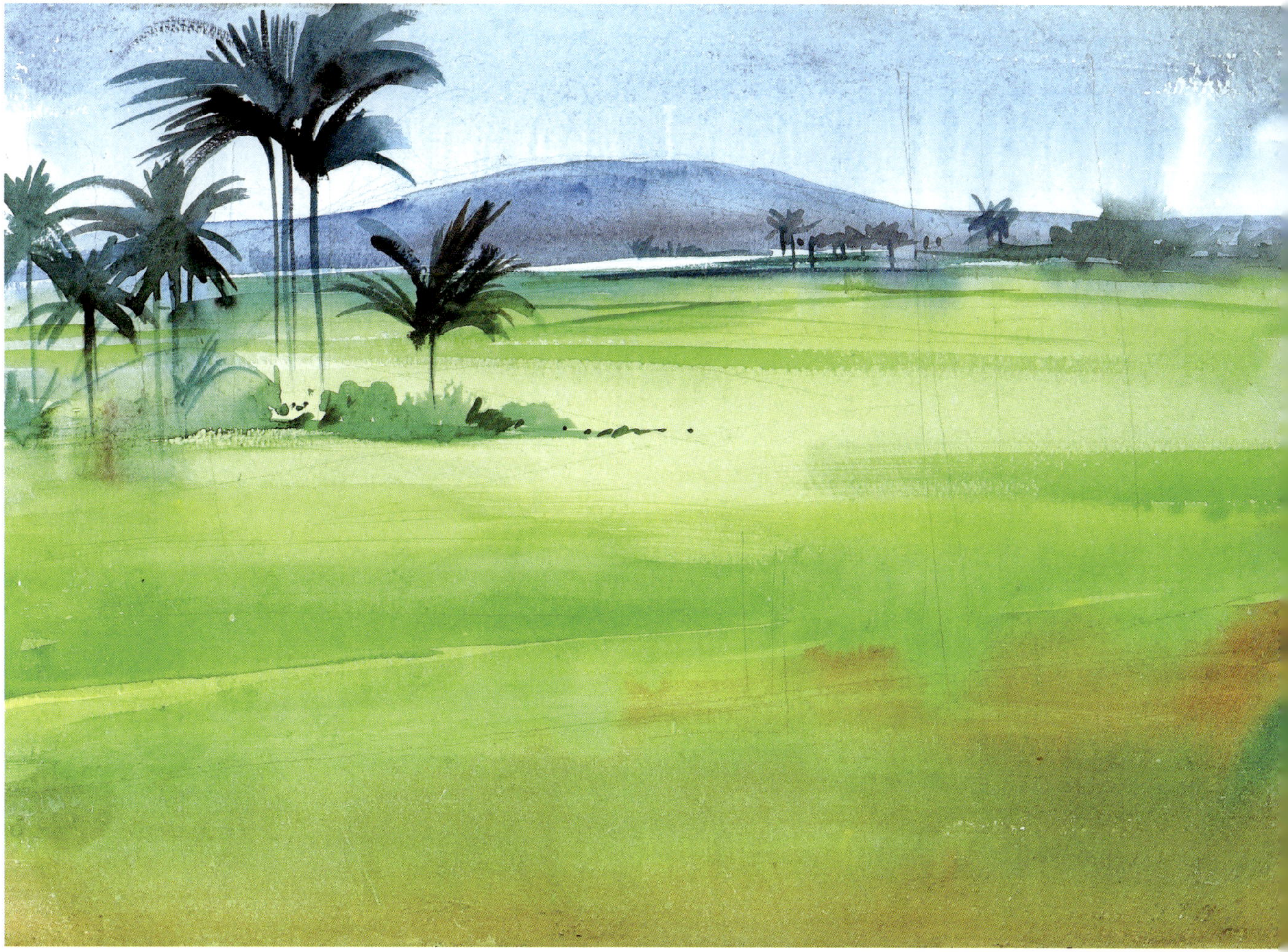

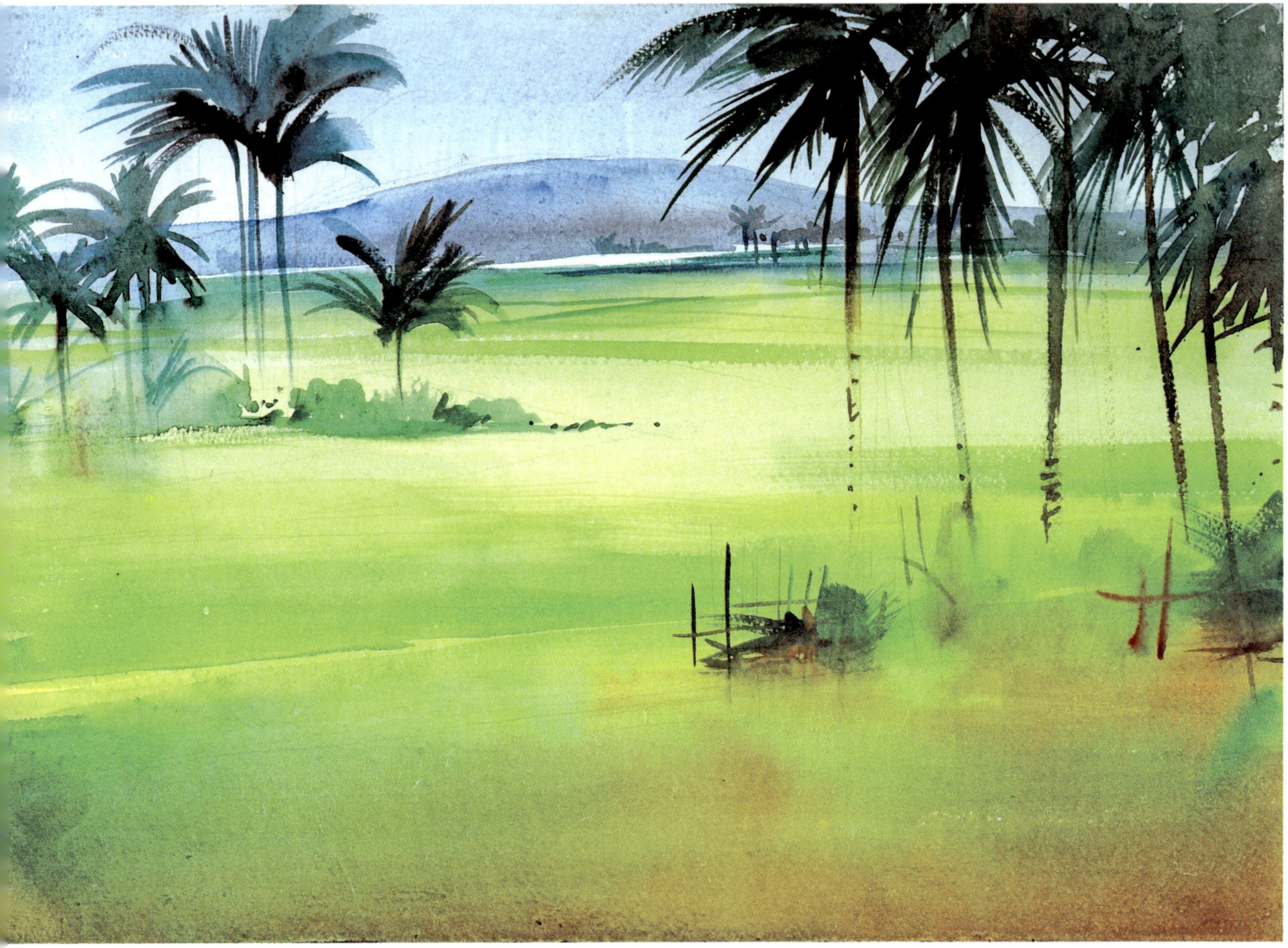

When all this was dry I used thick (cream) blue-green for the foreground coconut trees which have added a feeling of depth. The finer details were added last with a dry brush.

All the fresh, bright tones in this painting have been possible due to the superimposition of washes. The only precaution required is to move the brush lightly so as not to disturb the underlying layer.

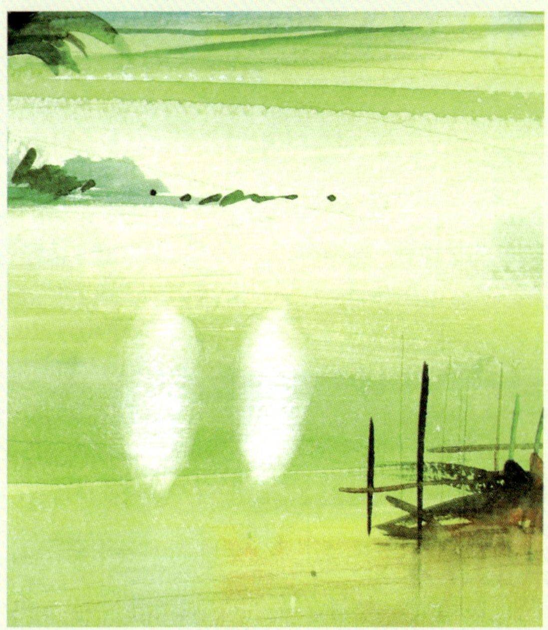

To show the two figures I applied a wet brush lightly over the first wash. Then I dabbed it with tissue paper to lift off some of the paint. This technique is called 'lifting'.

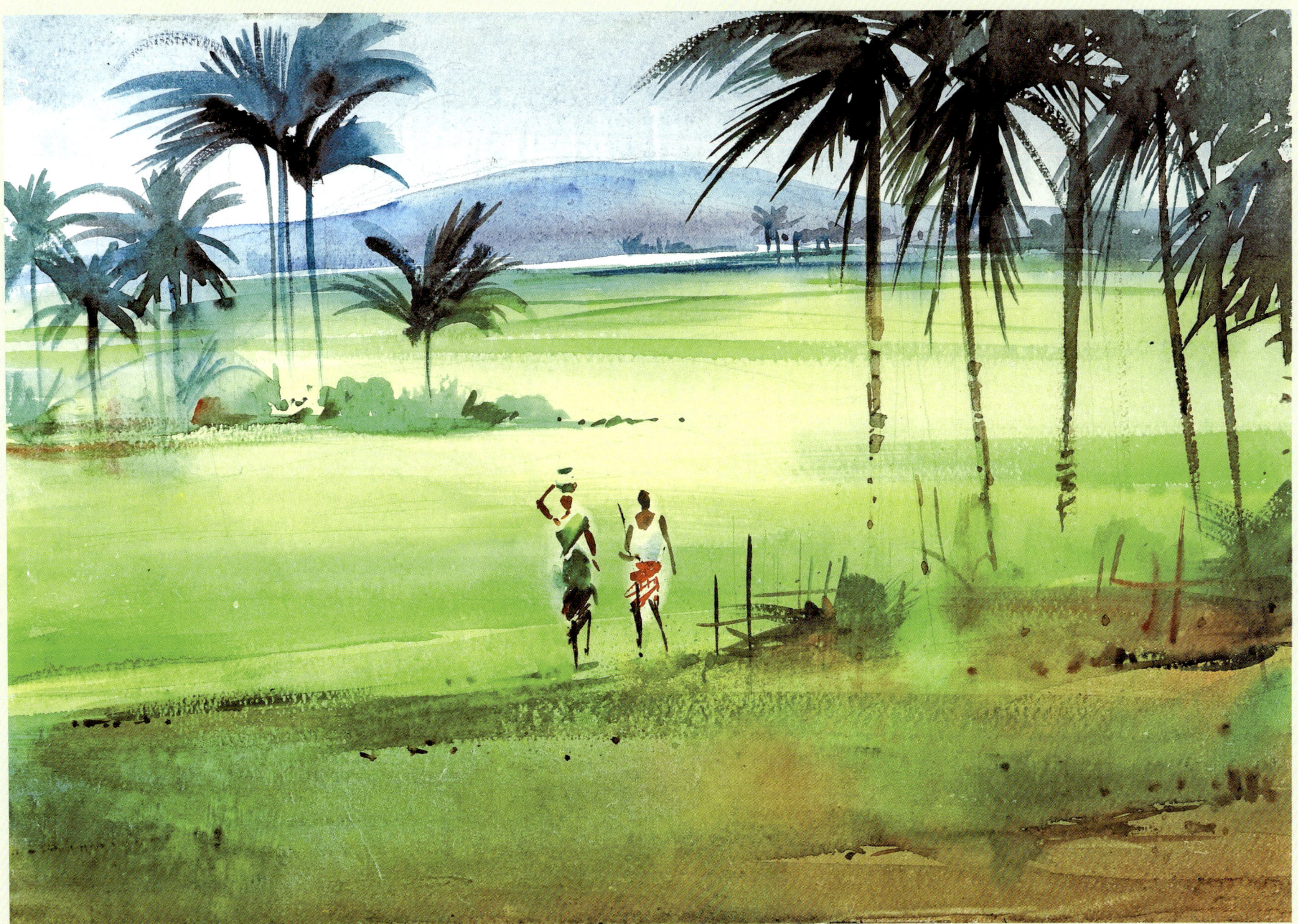

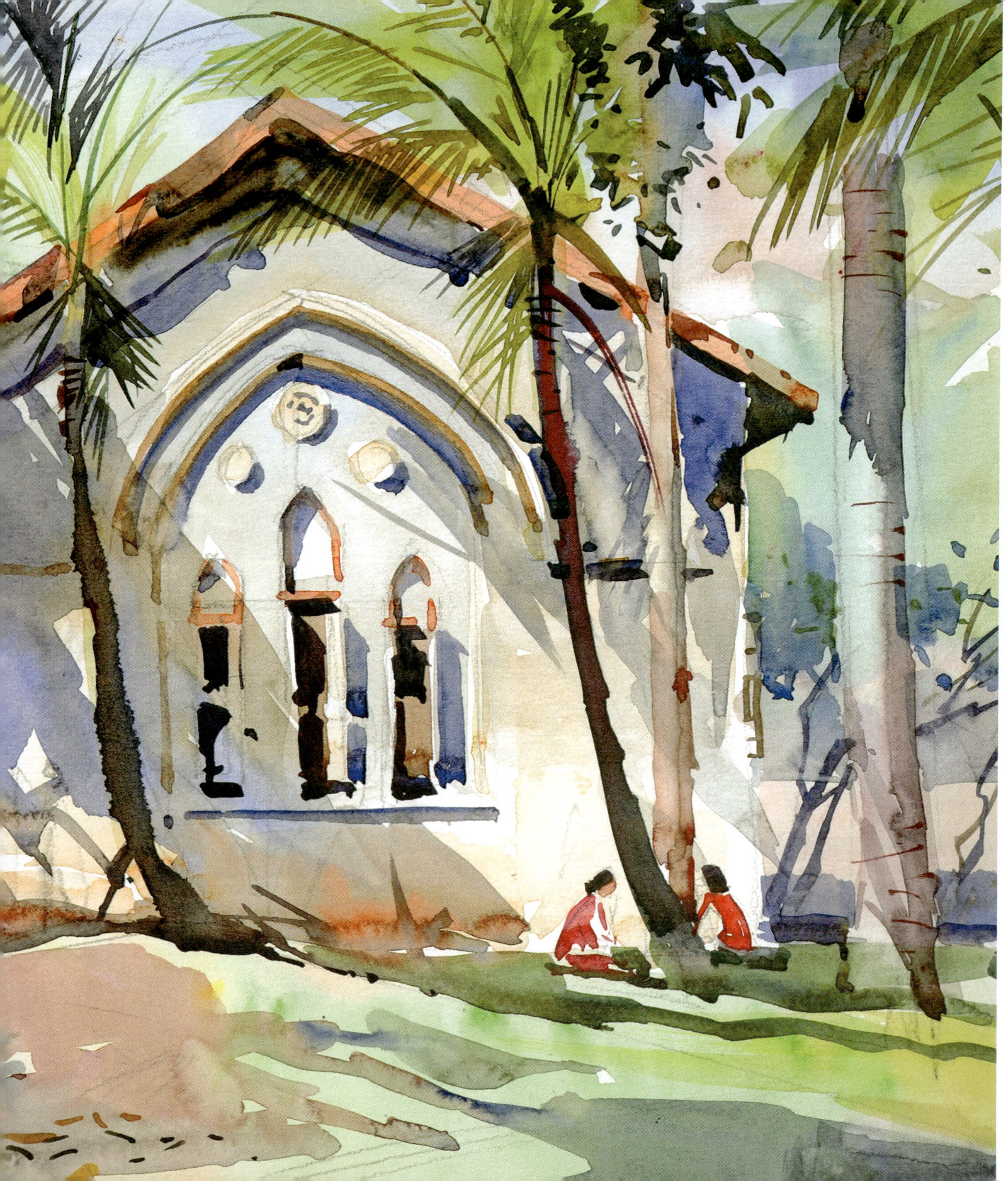

Assignment Four

Take simple subjects and practice glazing. Start with dilute paint and move on to thicker, darker paint. Apply four to five washes over one another. Compare the resulting dark tone with one got by painting a dark colour in one layer only. Try painting shadows with different shades using glazing. Use the painting on page 32-33 for reference.

While glazing, we keep applying one wash over the other as required.While working delicately, we hit upon the right colour and tone; along with this we also keep working on the forms and finalise them. While doing this, we build up the painting, leaving blurred margins in some places and sharpening the edges in precise areas.

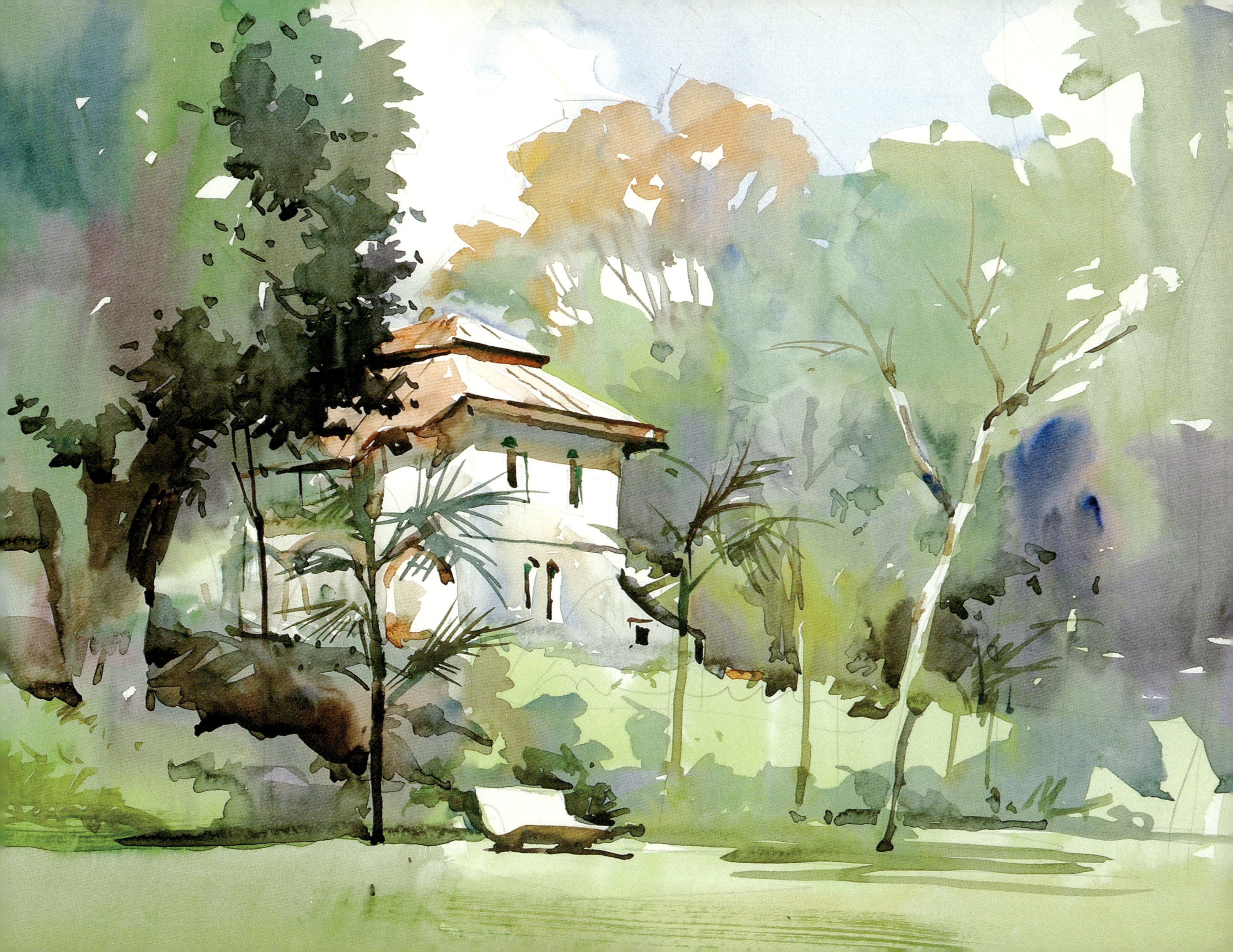

Wet-in-Wet Glazing 1

We often come across a beautiful and convincing depiction of fog or a rainy atmosphere in paintings. We realize that many layers of paint have been applied; yet we see no distinct edges anywhere. The colours too are of varying thickness. So how come the colours have not got hopelessly mixed up although the paper has been wet? This awesome skill is actually the result of wet-in-wet glazing.

In this technique we give a wash and allow each wash to dry completely as before. But before the next layer (wash) is applied the paper is again made wet with water. This process is repeated 3 or 4 times. This way we get the effect of blurred edges without the colours having mixed with each other. Let us learn more through this demonstration.

There is a curved road with trees on either side. It has just stopped raining and two figures are walking in the distance.

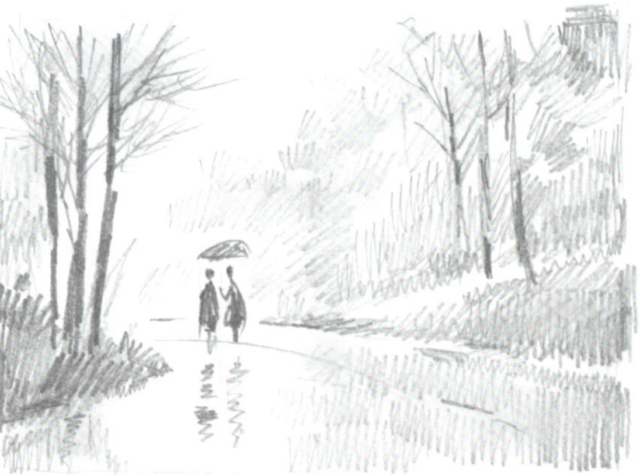

First I drew the outline of the trees and the road. Then leaving the area of the road untouched I wet the entire paper. Now, I let some light pink and blue flow onto the wet paper, leaving alone the area of the sky. This was to depict the distant trees.

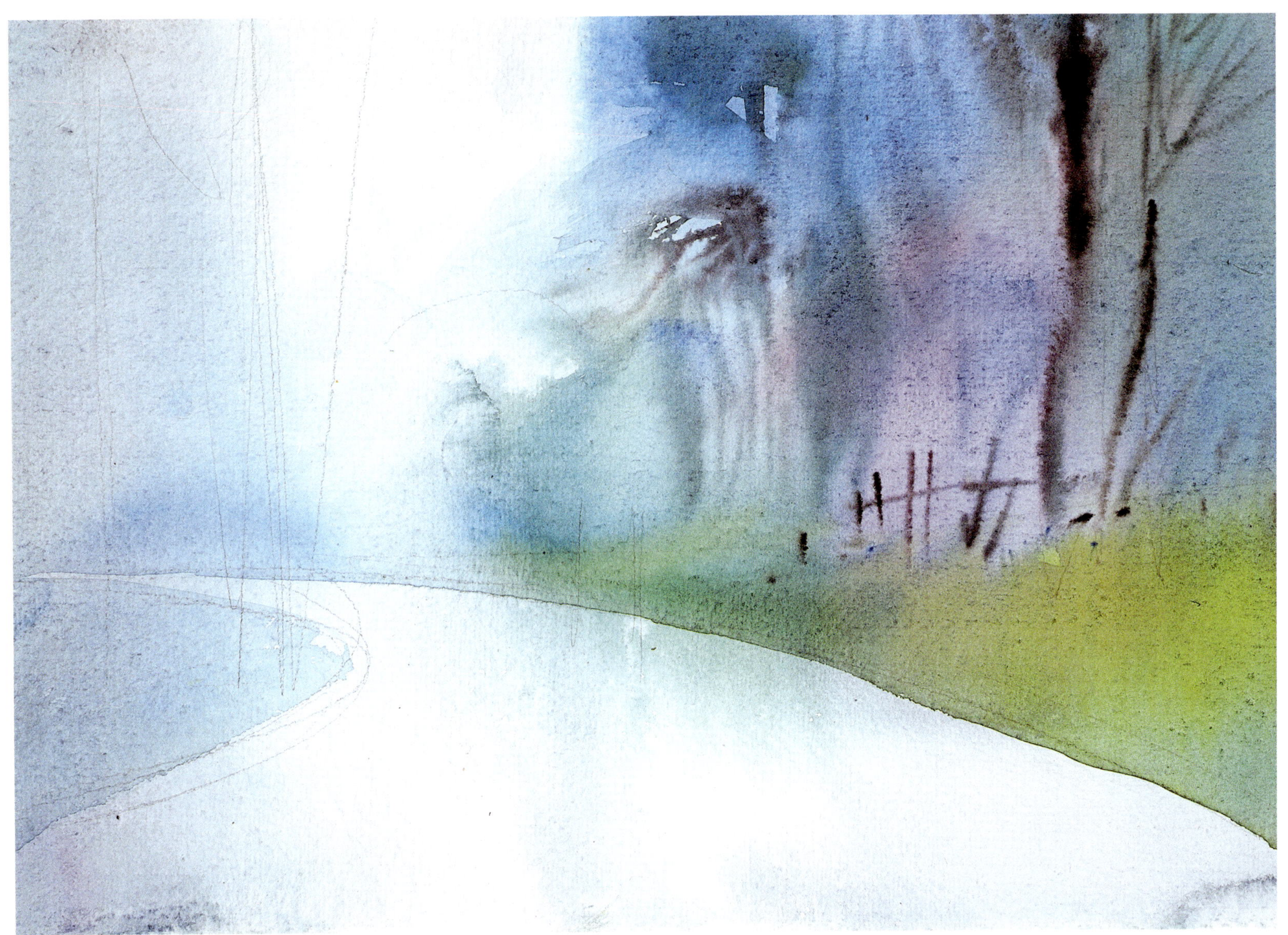

After this had dried I applied water once more. Now I used thicker and darker paint (milk) to show the foreground foliage.

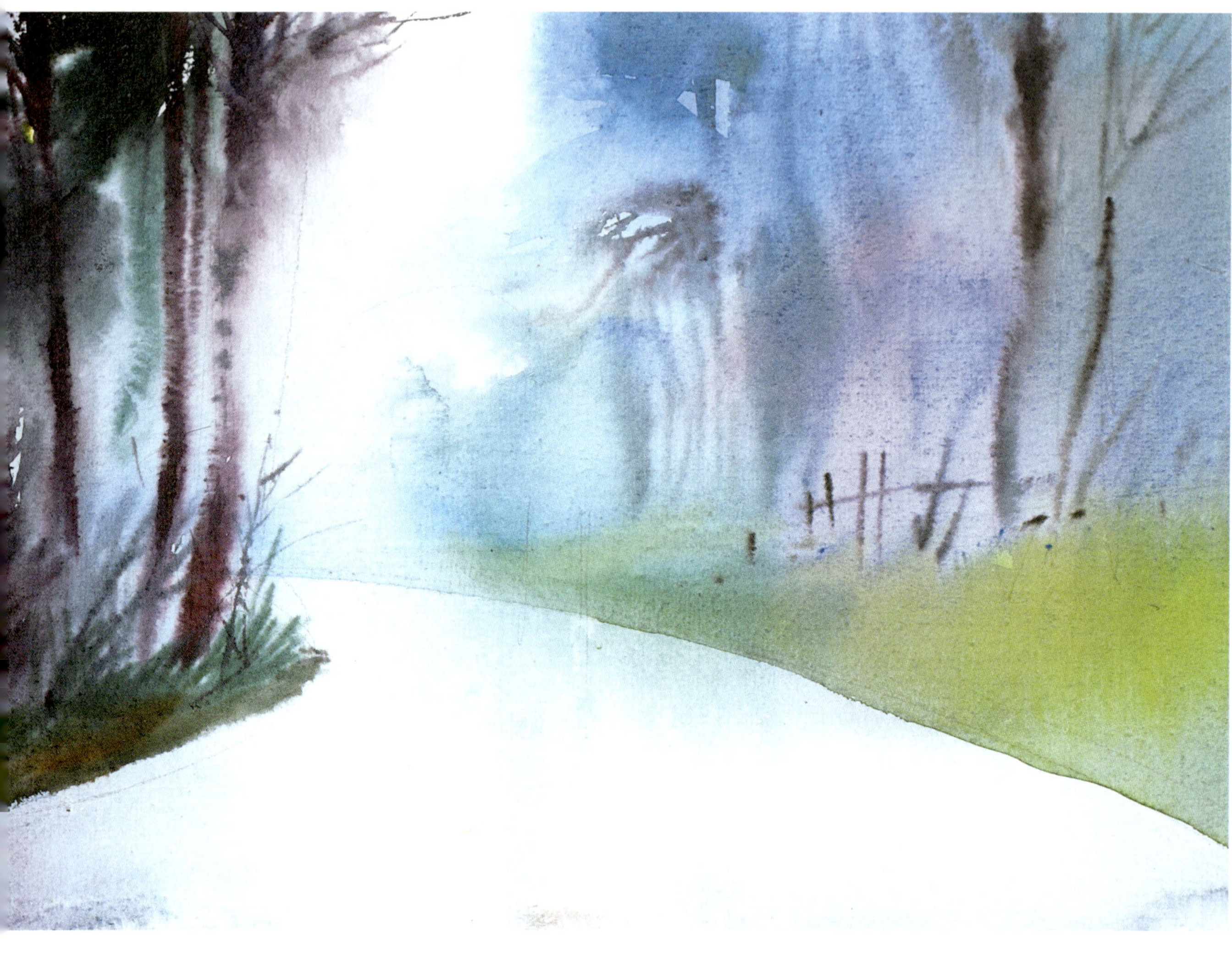

In the next step, after the earlier work was dry, I applied water once again. Then I showed the tree trunks using even darker and thicker paint. Every application of paint was on wet paper so there have been no sharp edges anywhere.

The same treatment was given to the road, but in two layers only. Care was taken to see that no dark paint was applied in areas where the light of the sky was reflected on the road. Finally the figures were drawn with thick paint.

Once you have gained good control over wet-in-wet glazing, then depicting the effect of fog or rainy atmosphere will come easily to you.

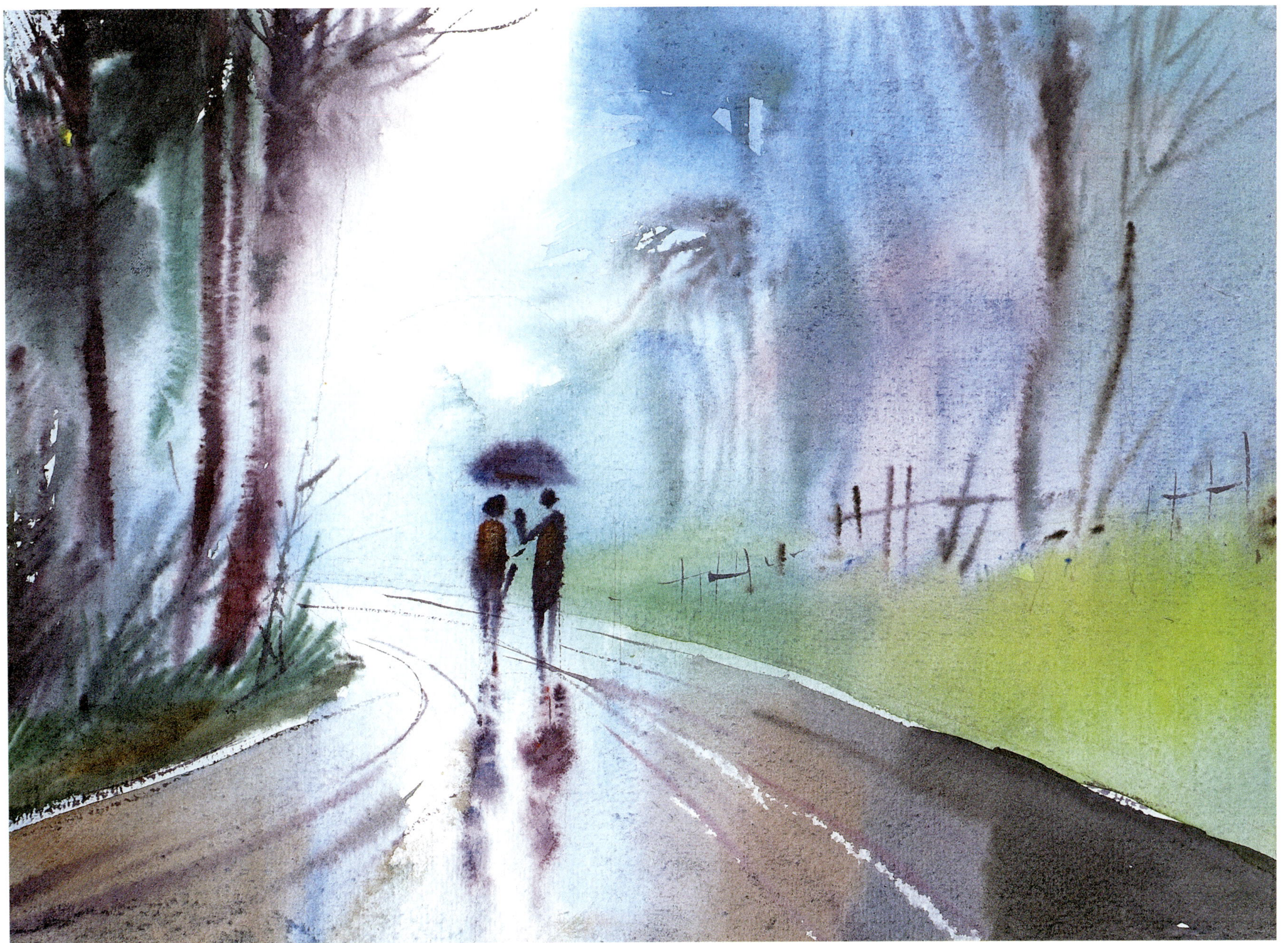

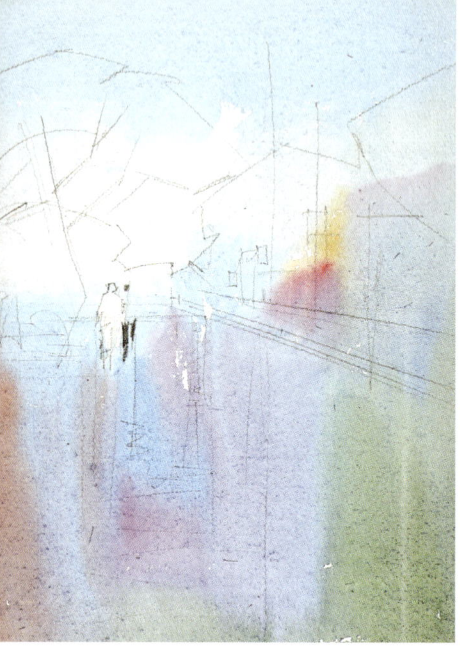

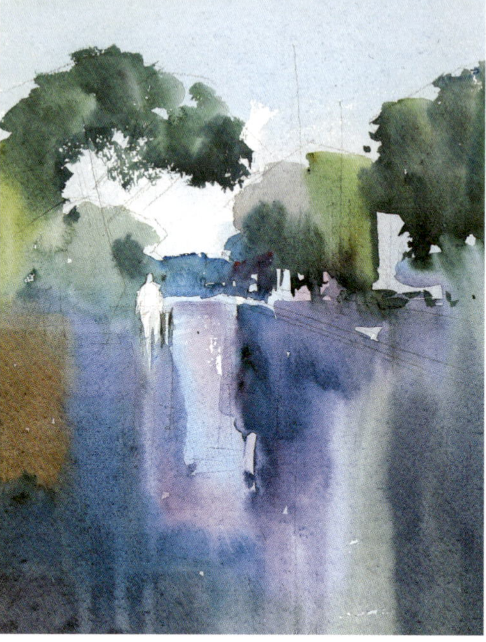

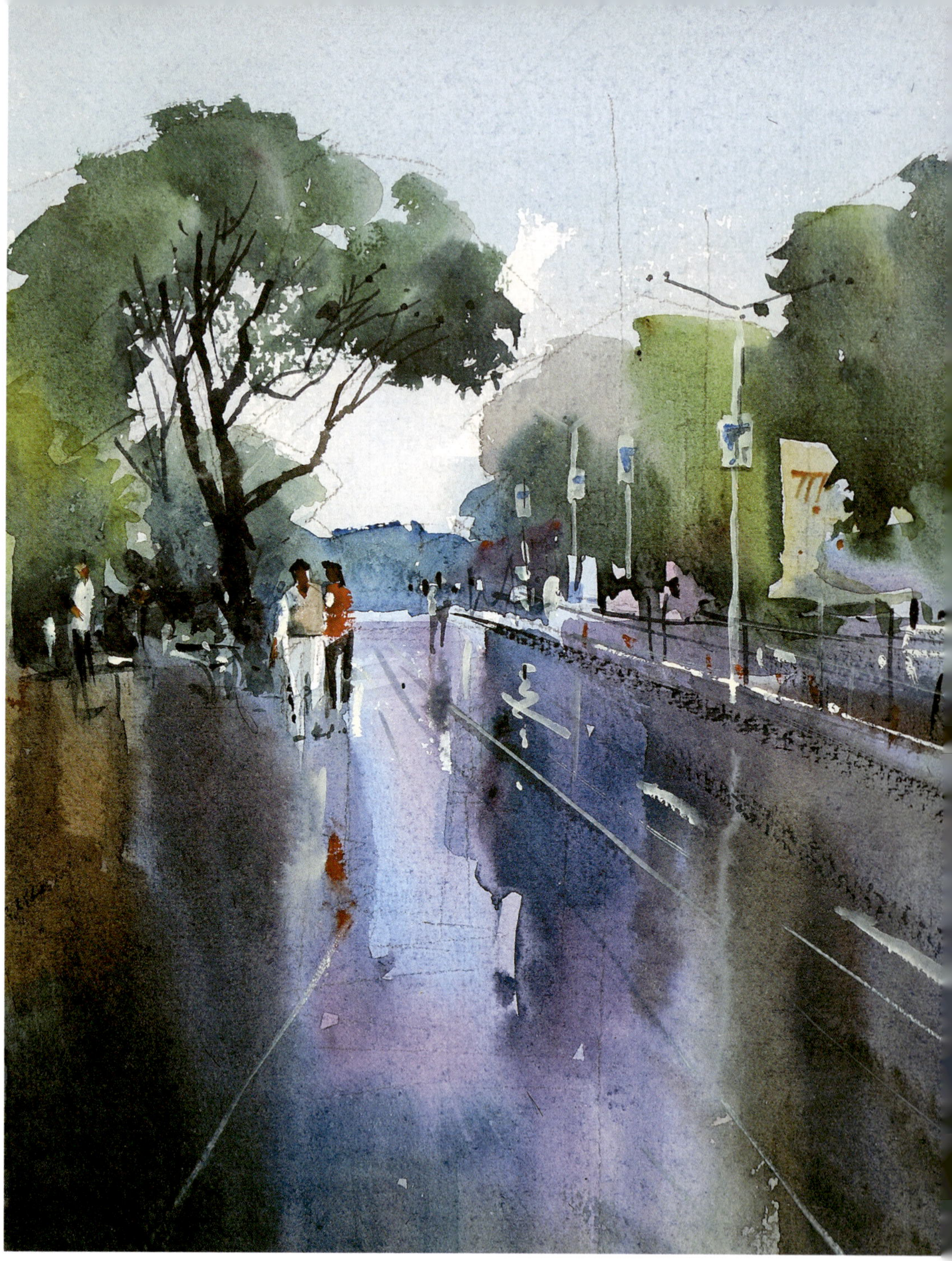

Sometimes though, you may want some sharp edges too along with the merged effect. In such a situation you can wet only the required area and apply paint there for a localized wet-in-wet effect. The same wash can then be extended onto the adjoining dry area for the desired sharp edges.

Assignment Five

While attempting this painting you may have got it right or you may have been totally demoralized.

When using wet-in-wet method, usually one is successful or the painting is a total failure. There is no middle stage. But do not lose hope. Try again using a photograph of a fog scene or any other similar painting. The only way to master the technique is practice.

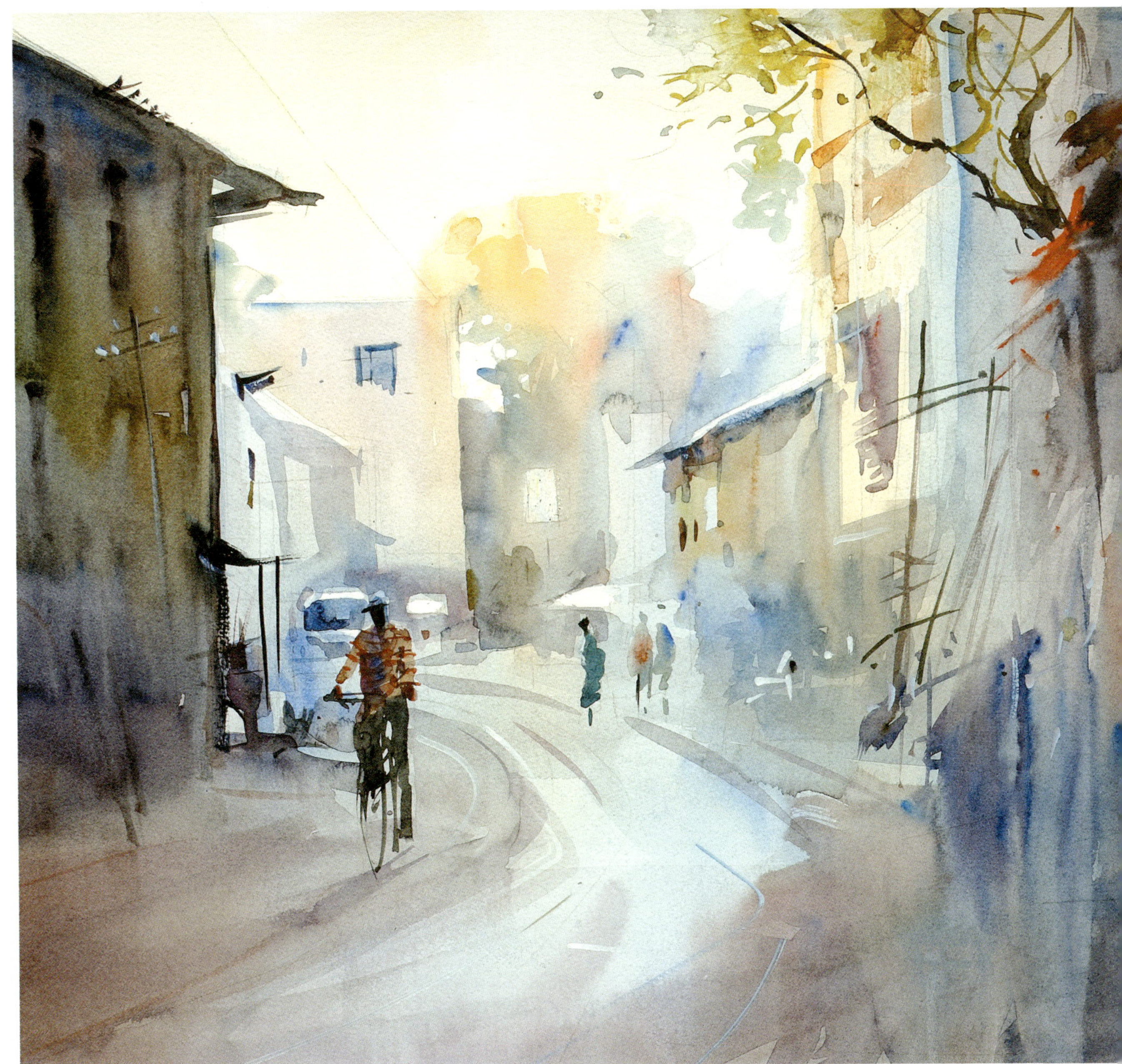

Wet-in-Wet Glazing 2

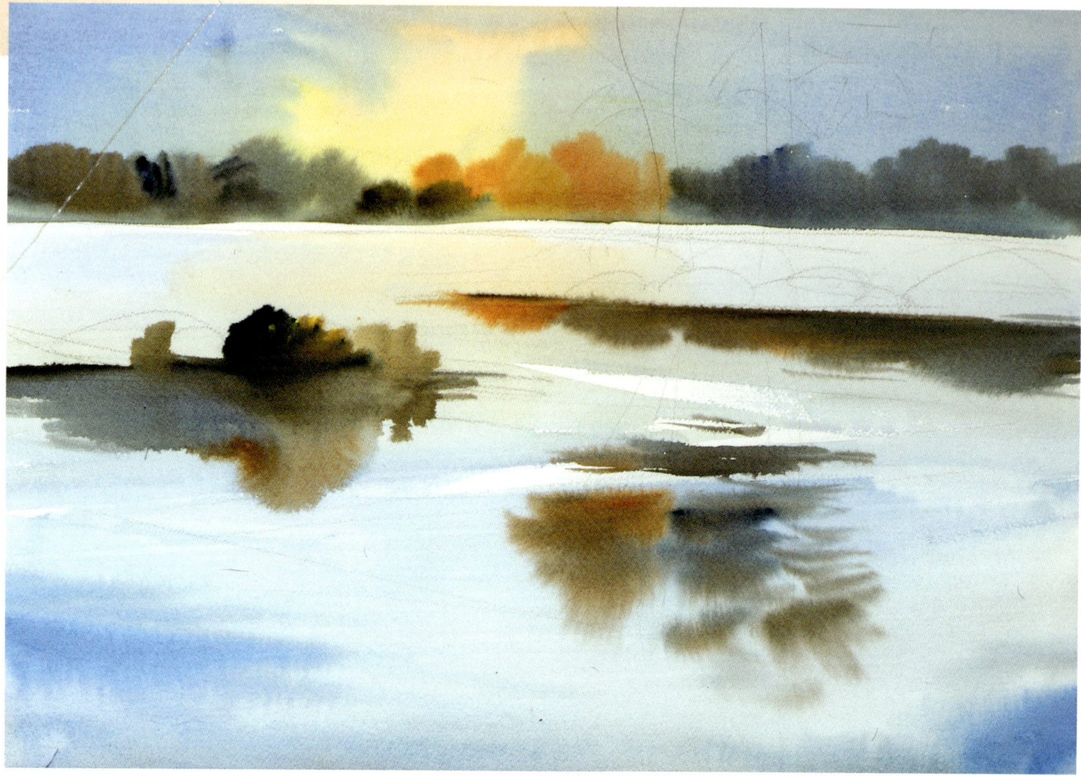

We have seen how to get blurred edges by wetting the paper over and over after the initial layer has dried.

Now the painting that we are going to attempt has some areas done on dry paper and other areas are to be done after wetting the paper. So, some areas will be blurred while others will be sharp.

The adjoining sketch shows an expanse of water with distant foliage. There are a couple of small islands with some shrubbery. These islands and the shrubs have cast reflections in the water. The setting is of an evening.

The sky has been done in a mixture of blue, purple and orange. While the wash was still wet the distant trees and foliage were done with thick paint. That meant that I got blurred edges. While painting the water similar colours were used. While applying this wash, an 'S' shaped area was left unpainted in the lower part, to depict the 'polished' and bright water surface. This is going to be the area to get the 'controlled' treatment.

When the whole paper was dry I wet it in places where I had shown the water. When still wet, I painted the reflections of the islands and their shrubs. To get the desired effect without sharp edges some practice is definitely required. This is because we have to finish applying paint before the paper dries up again.

When this second wash was dry, the shrubs were drawn according to their reflections painted in earlier. Here I got the desired sharp edges since the paper was dry. So finally we have a painting where some areas have sharp edges while others are blurred.

The reflections needed to be without sharp edges. Since we have little control over how paint behaves while working wet-in-wet, the reflections were done before doing the actual shrubs, on a dry surface.

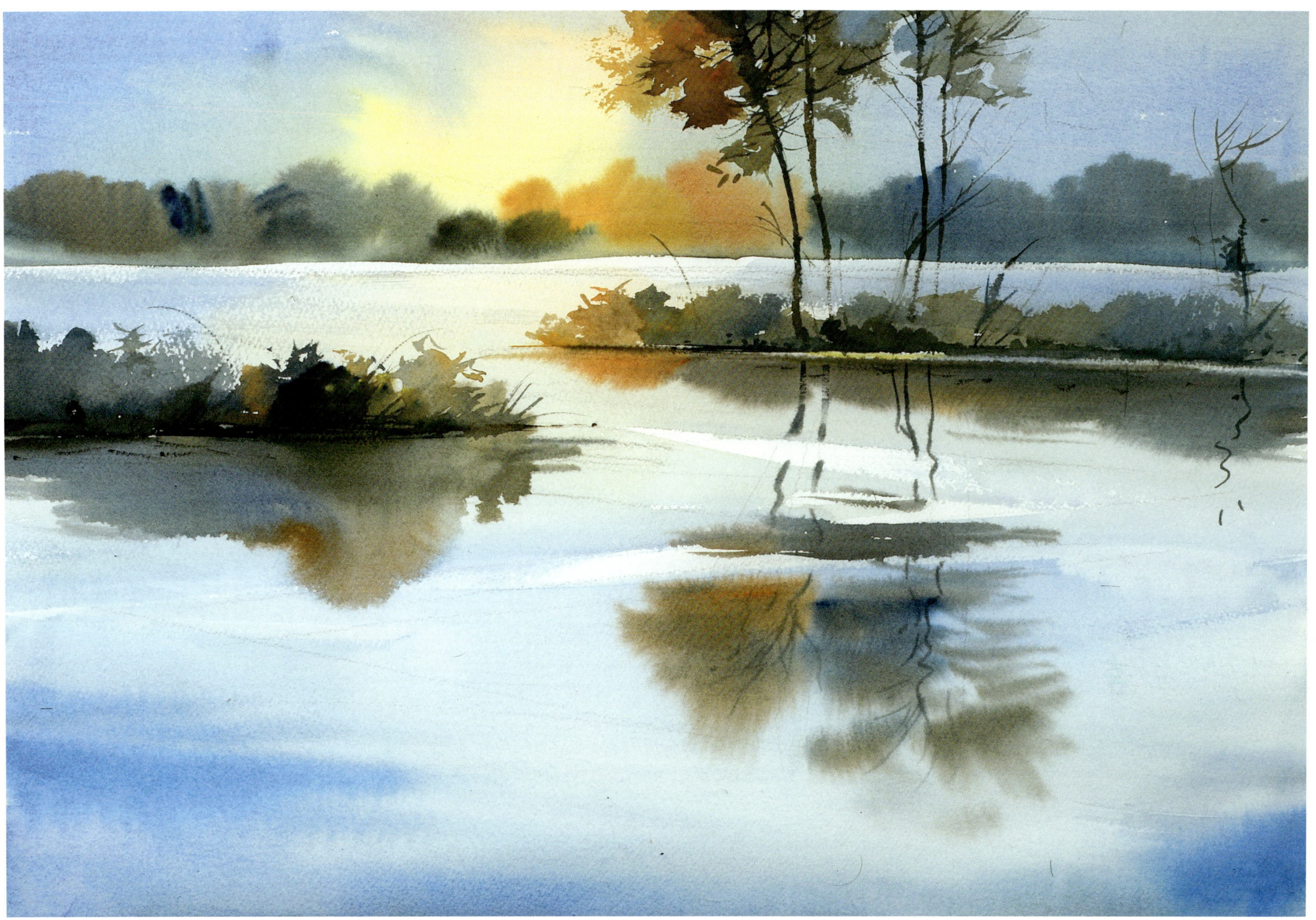

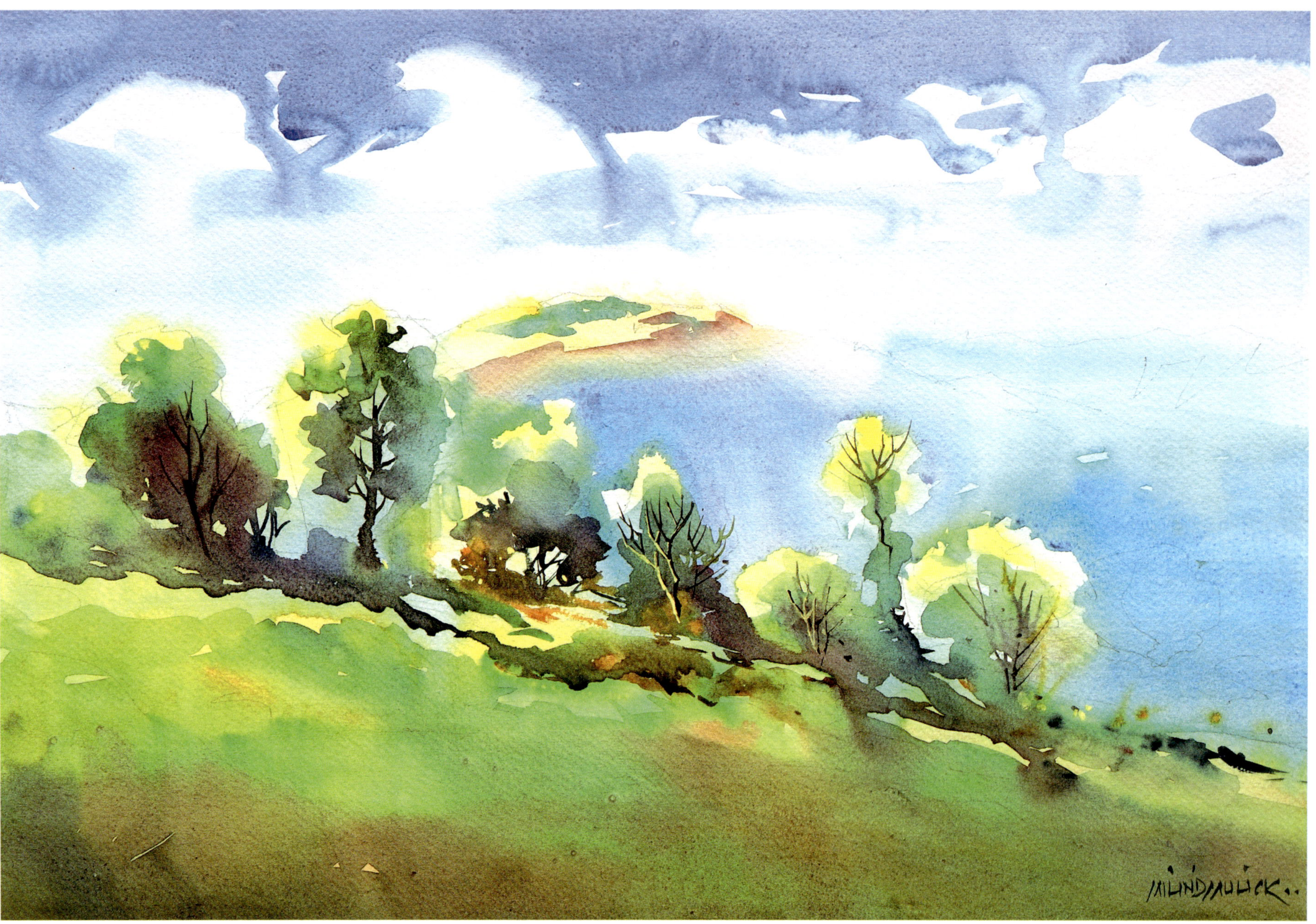

Assignment Six

Consider copying the paintings on pages 42-43 as an exercise. Keep on practising till you are satisfied. Then experiment with colours.

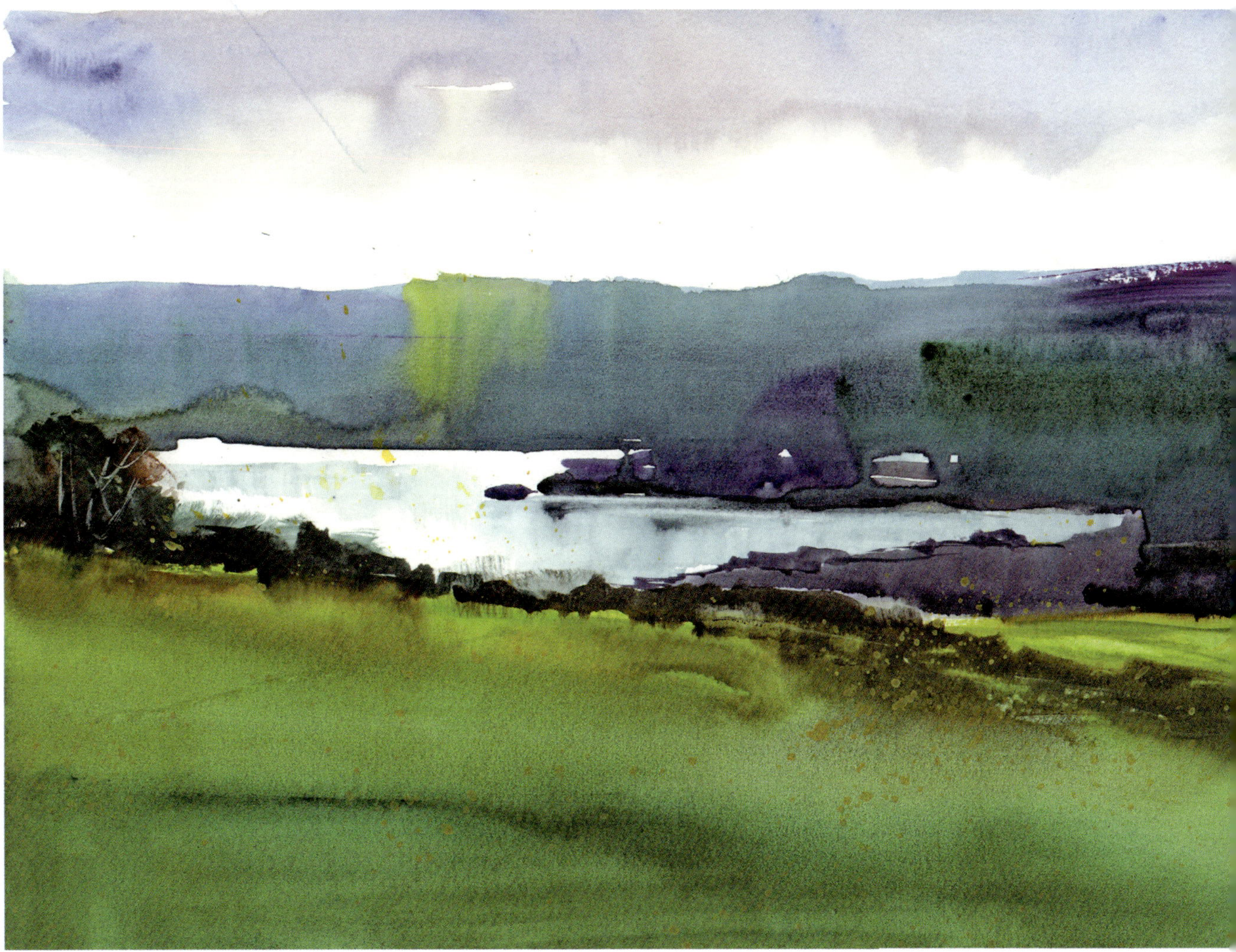

This painting has no object in it. I have tried to make an interesting composition by using a controlled wet-in-wet technique. Such a 'minimalist' approach is often effective in creating atmosphere.

We see various shapes in cloud formations. We have seen this as children. Yet we tend to show clouds having rounded edges when we paint. But to make clouds realistic, try different shapes.

Lesson Seven

Brushwork

What is brushwork? Obviously it is the depiction of forms by using the brush! The further from its tip we hold the brush in our hand, the easier will be the movement. In other words, we will have better control over it.

Generally when we depict grass or tree branches, we should be doing it in single strokes. This is called calligraphic brushwork.

I prefer doing bold patches rather than delicate detailing, giving importance to the play of light and shadows on the objects. There is not much of tonal variation in such brushwork.

It is worth practising a variety of shapes before going for the actual painting. Once you gain control over brushwork, you would be able to become free with your washes. Even a 'wrong' wash can be corrected by suitable brushwork later, and still keeping the painting under control.

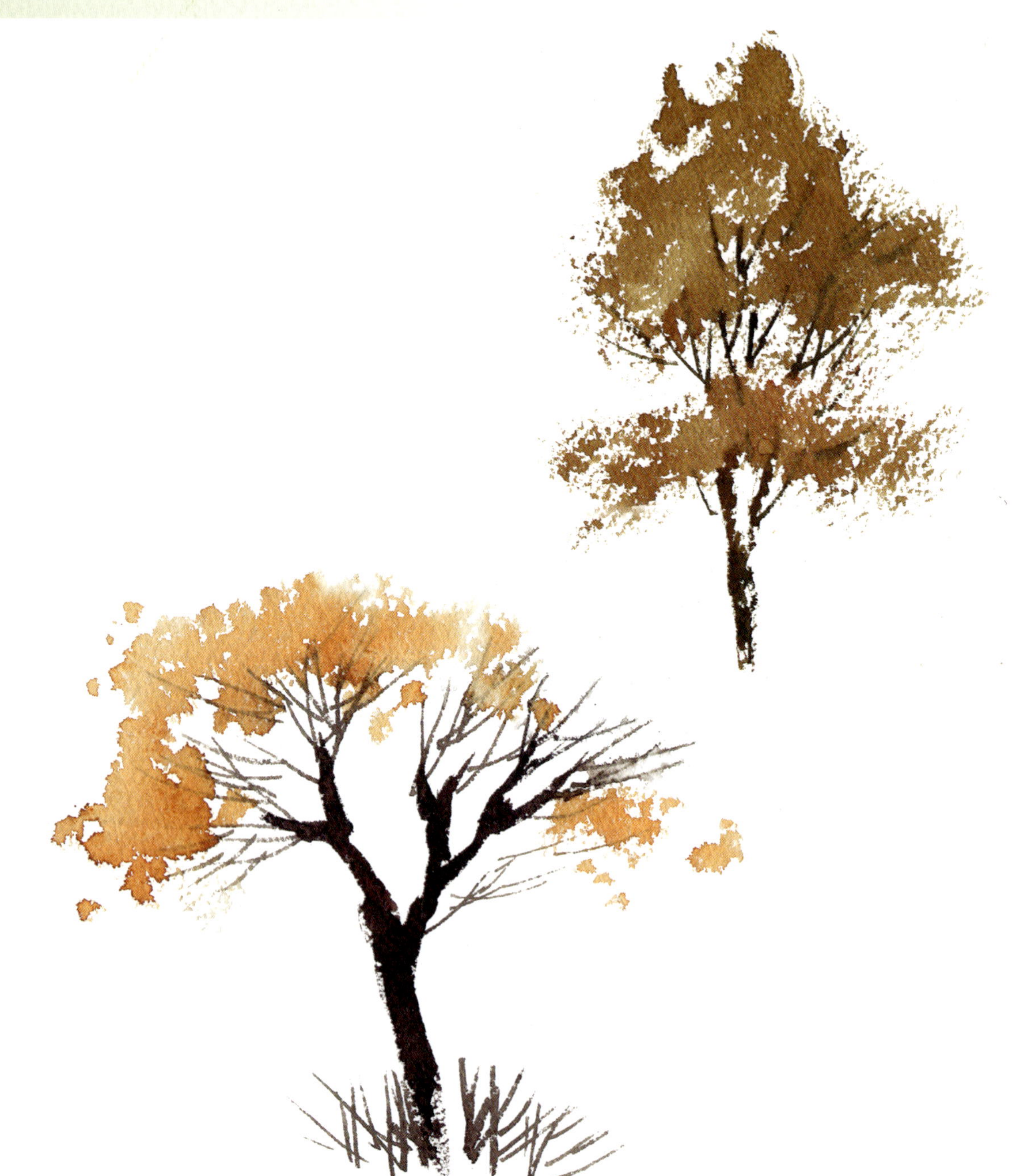

Brushwork involves practice to the eyes too. So it is preferable to go outdoors. Observe how coconut fronds are different from palm, how banyan and mango trees are different, how trees appear in a 'mass' and so on. As you observe carefully and practice, it will show in your brushwork.

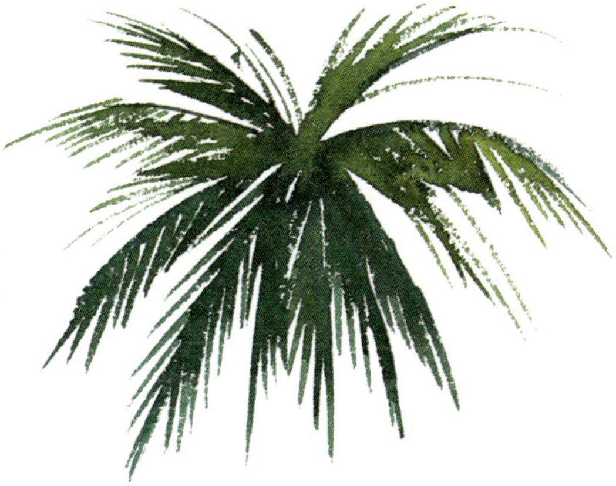

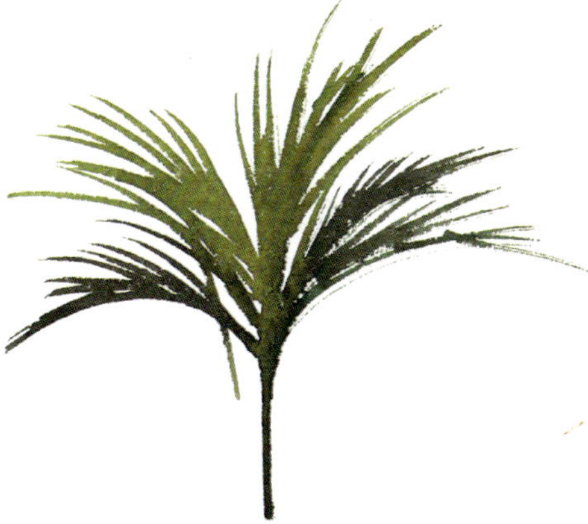

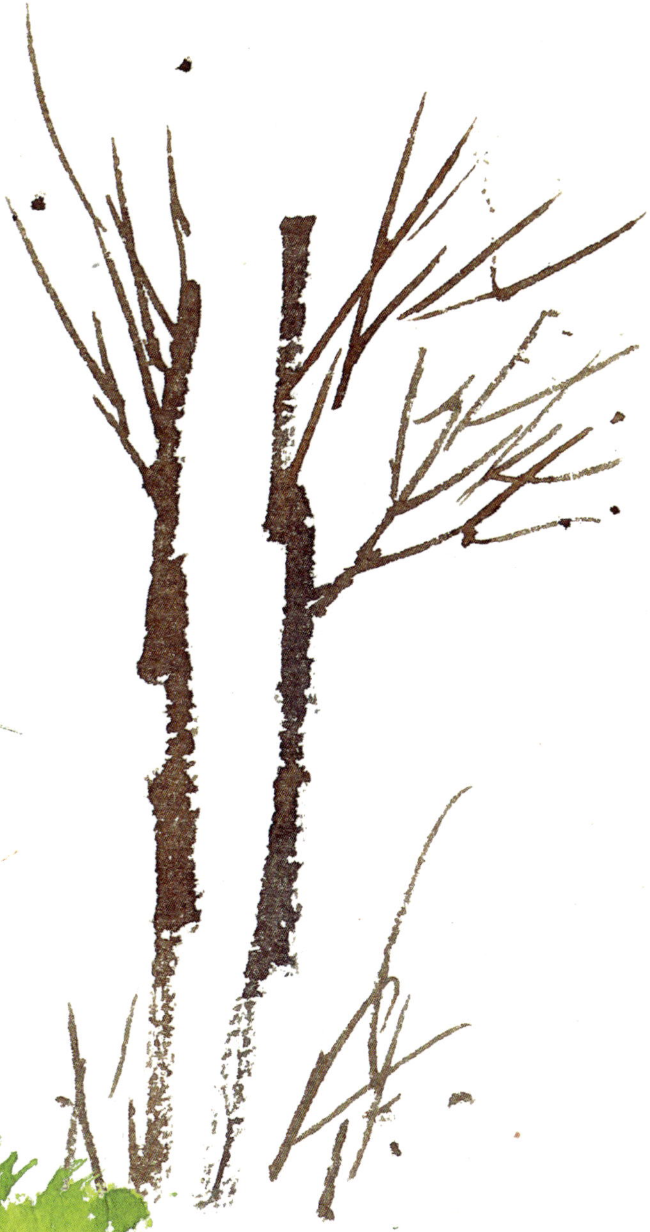

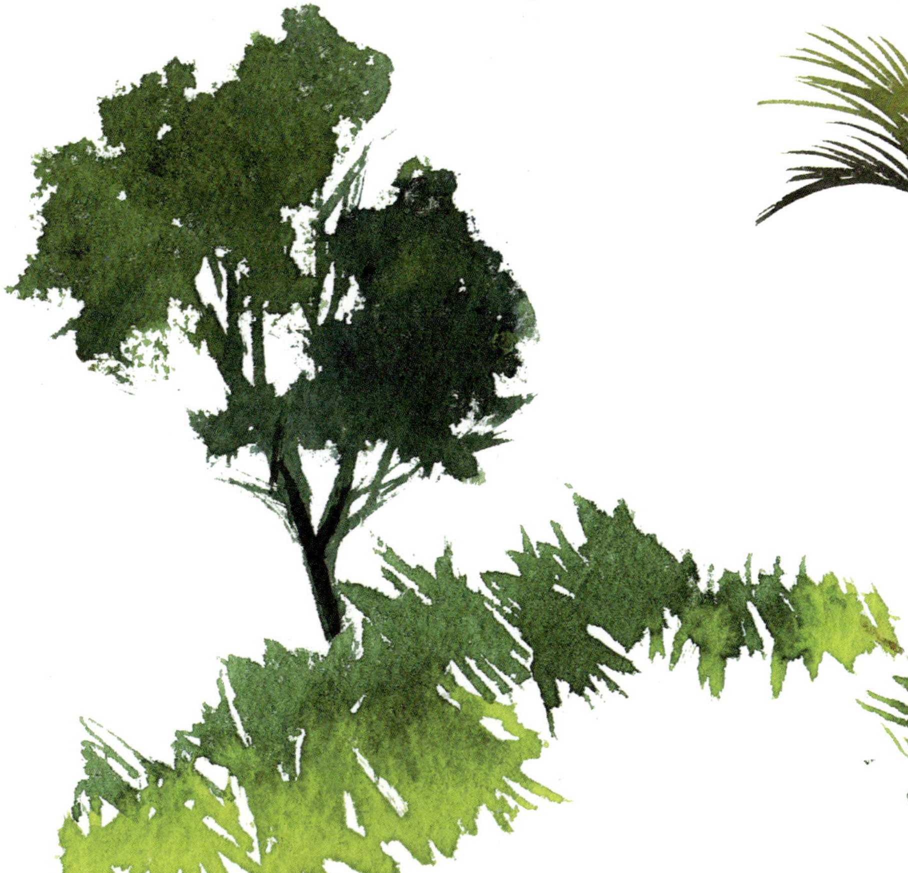

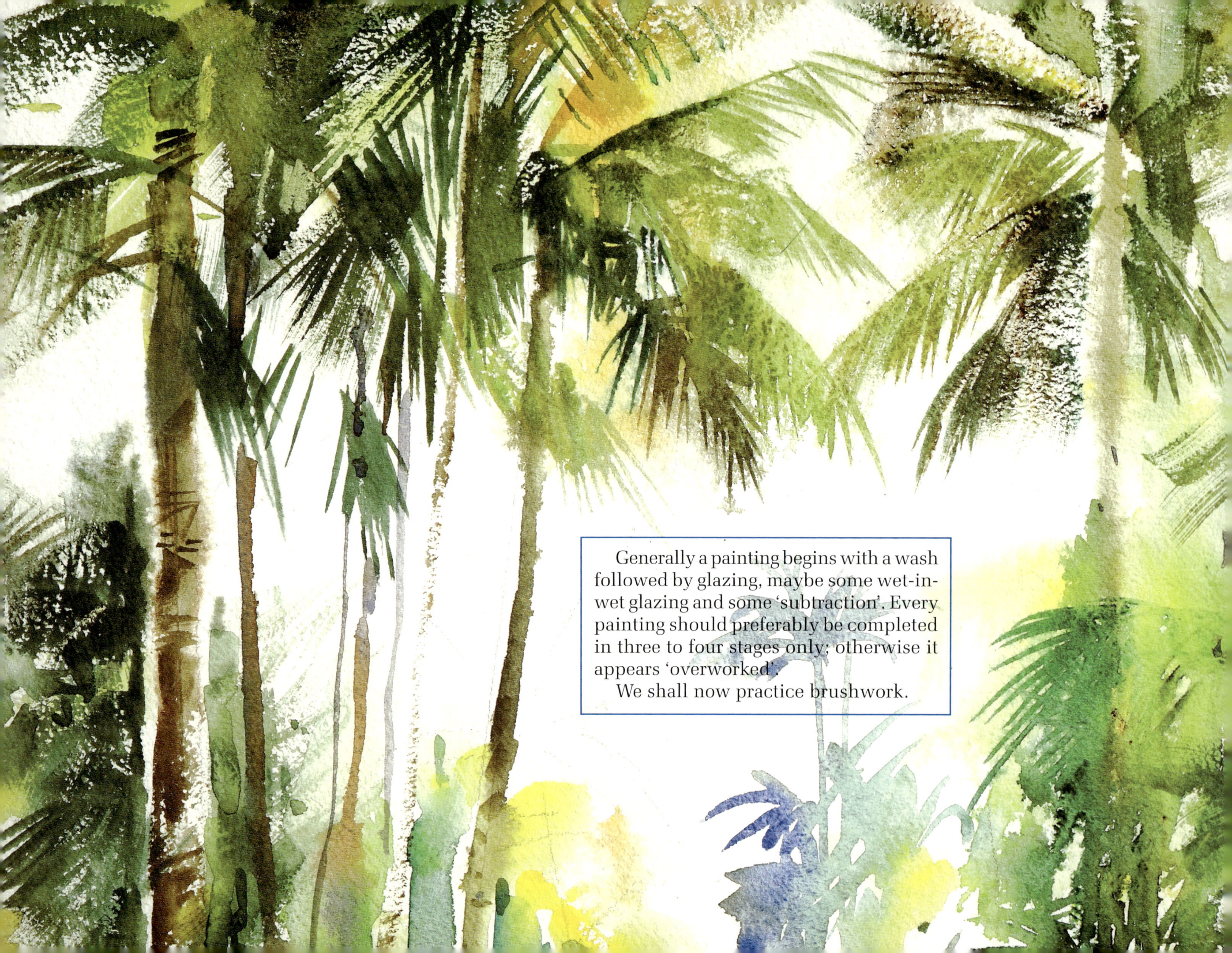

Generally a painting begins with a wash followed by glazing, maybe some wet-in-wet glazing and some 'subtraction'. Every painting should preferably be completed in three to four stages only; otherwise it appears 'overworked'.

We shall now practice brushwork.

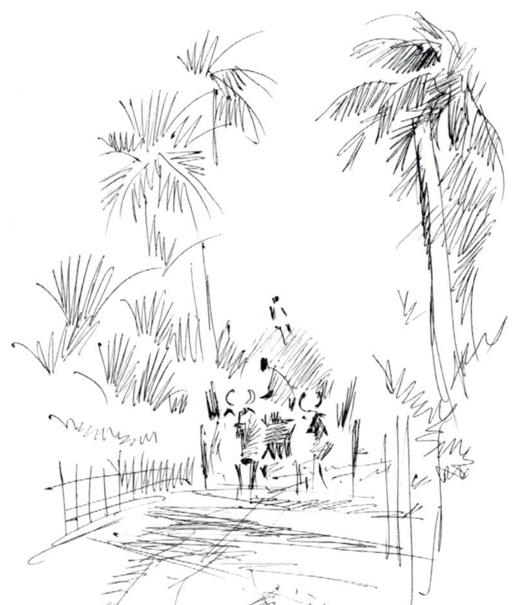

A bullock-cart is approaching us along a well-shaded road, in a typical Konkan scene. Don't be overwhelmed by the thought of painting a bullock-cart. It is actually quite easy to draw bullocks in a front view.

Leaving the part of the bullock-cart untouched I painted the sky with blue, the foliage in various shades of green and the road in a mixture of orange and crimson. I allowed the colours to mix as in a variegated wash.

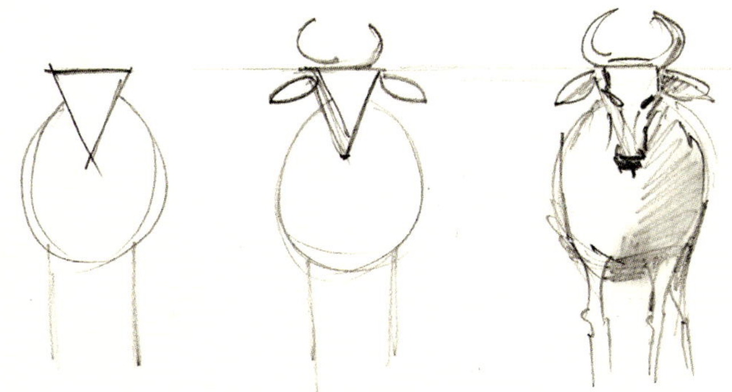

A triangle, a circle and two legs! Just take care to draw the circle in the right place.

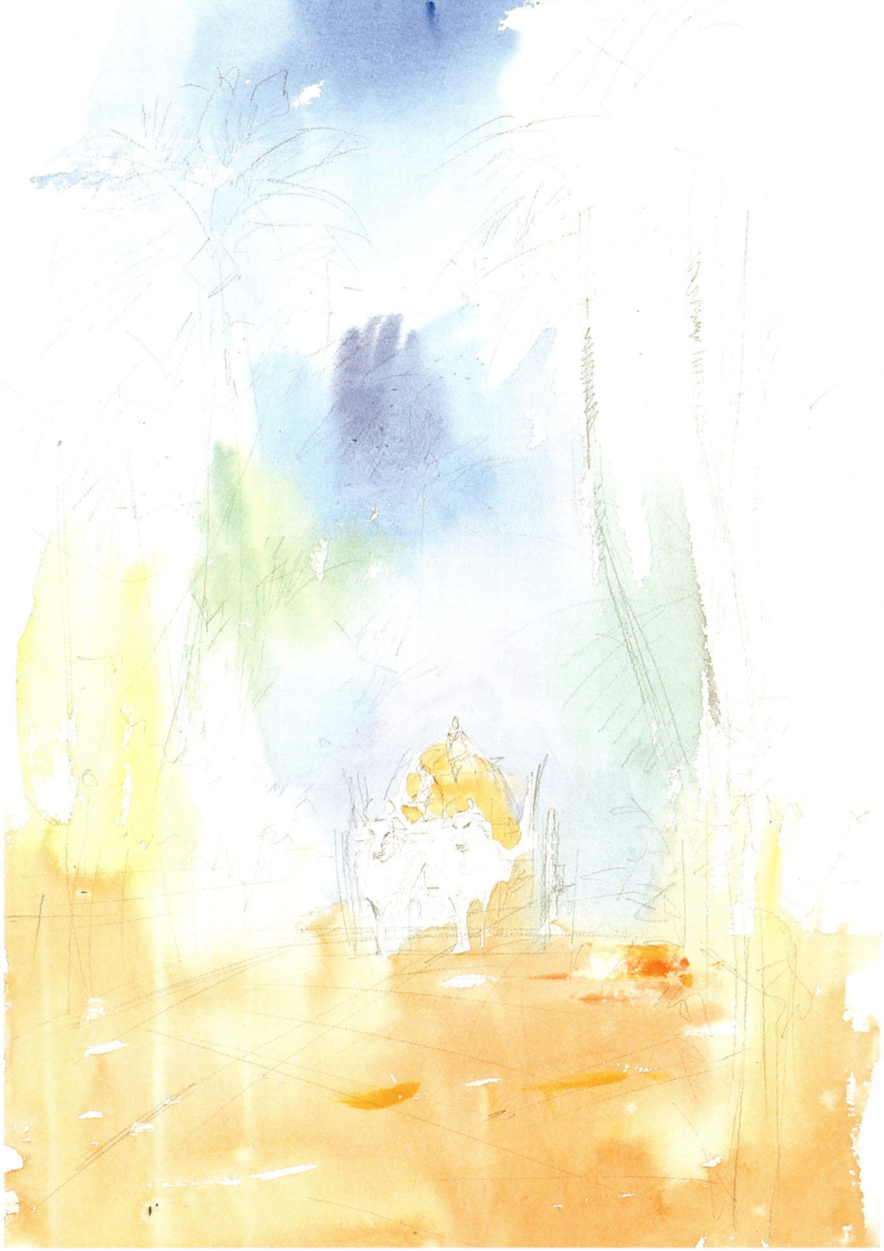

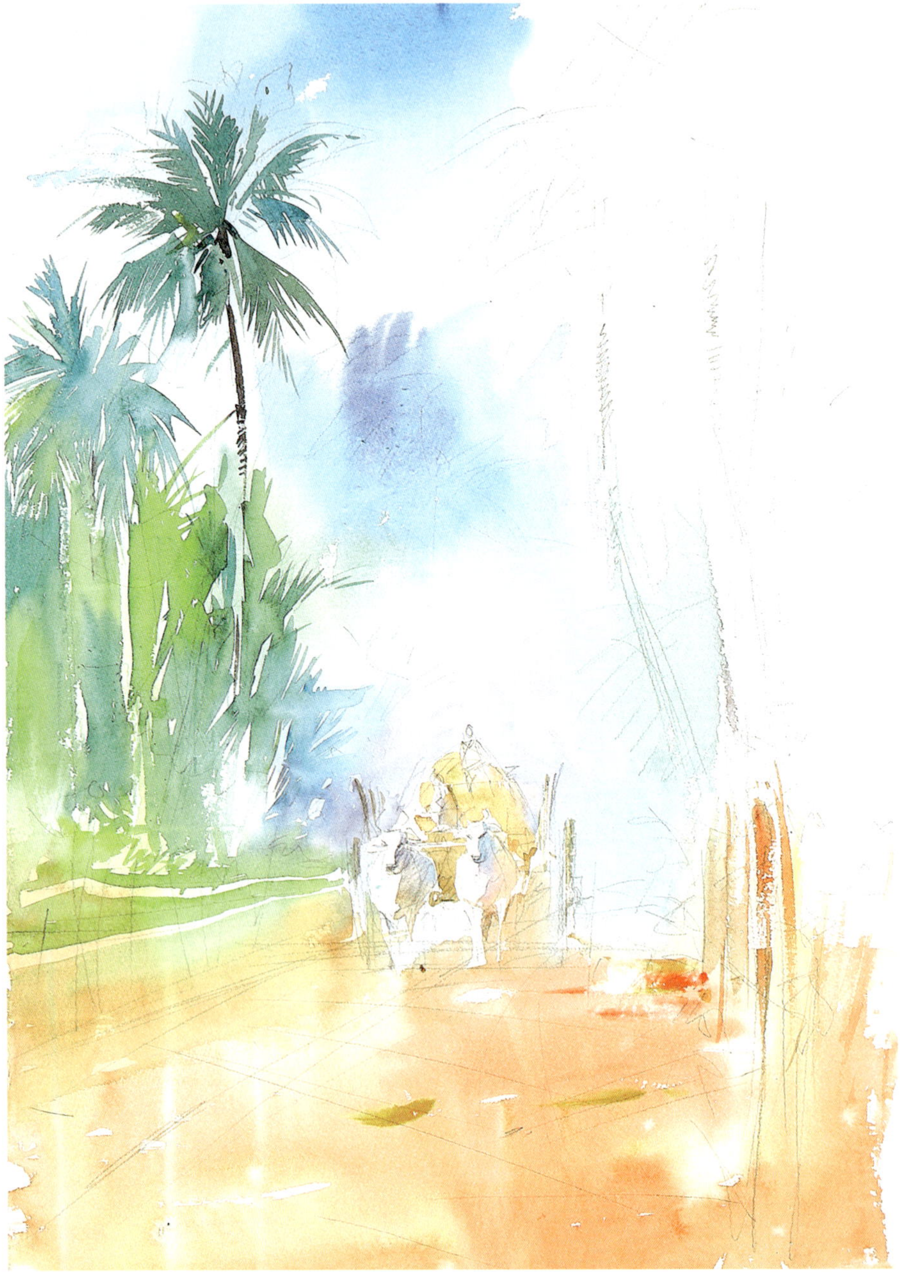

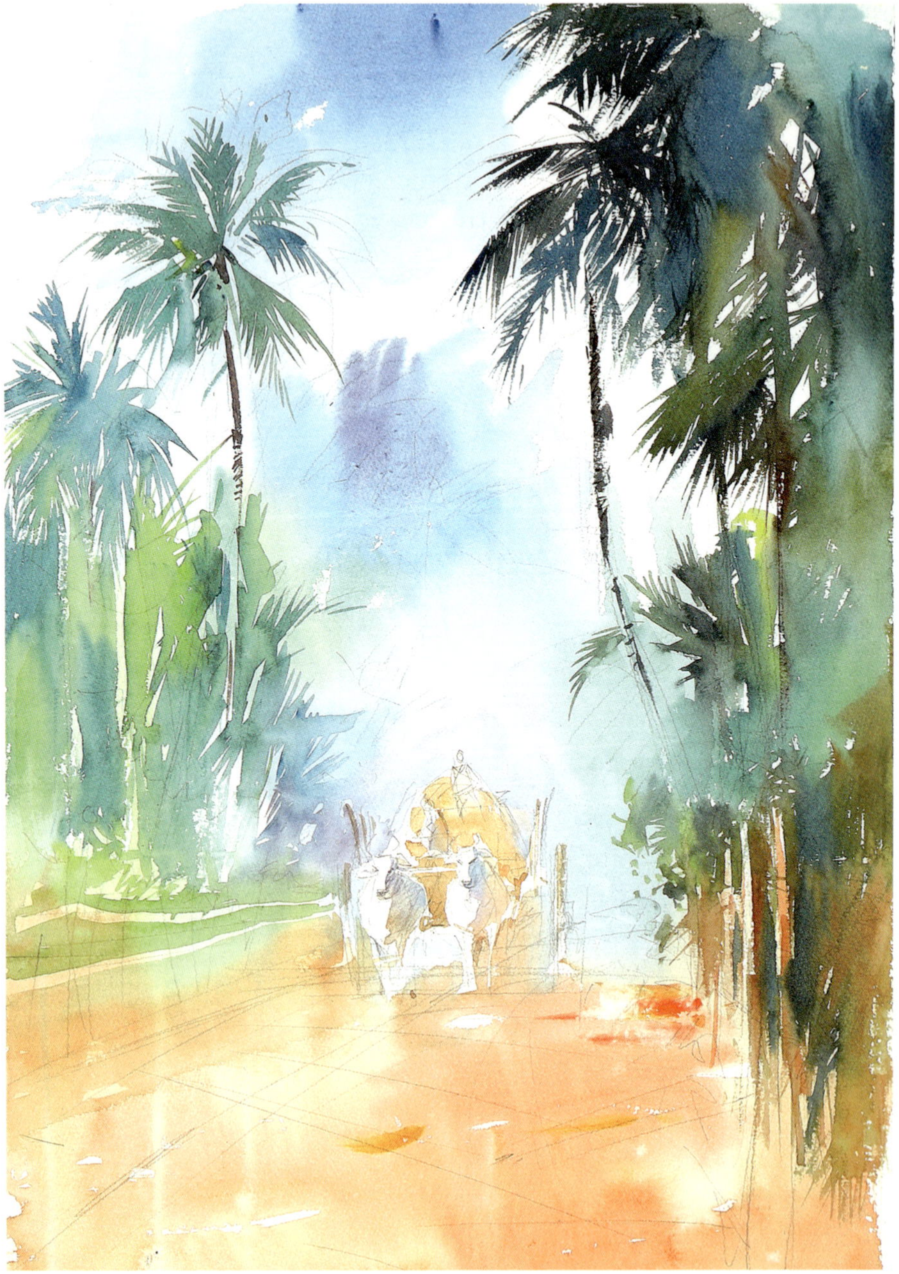

The bullock-cart will require some careful handling. First I painted the bales of grass in it with light yellow-orange. The bullocks' backs were done in cobalt blue plus orange, taking care to leave some unpainted patches to give the effect of sunlit areas.

Once these steps had dried our real brushwork will begin. In this painting it is the brushwork that 'holds' the picture together.

The fronds of the coconut trees, their trunks, the shrubs and the shadows across the road have all been done in bold, single strokes. There is 'force' in this painting because no stroke was repeated or worked upon beyond the initial application. Even the wheels of the cart, the figures, the legs of the bullocks and the fence posts have been painted in single strokes. An illusion of detail has been achieved with the minimum of appropriate strokes.

Needless to say, practice is *the* key.

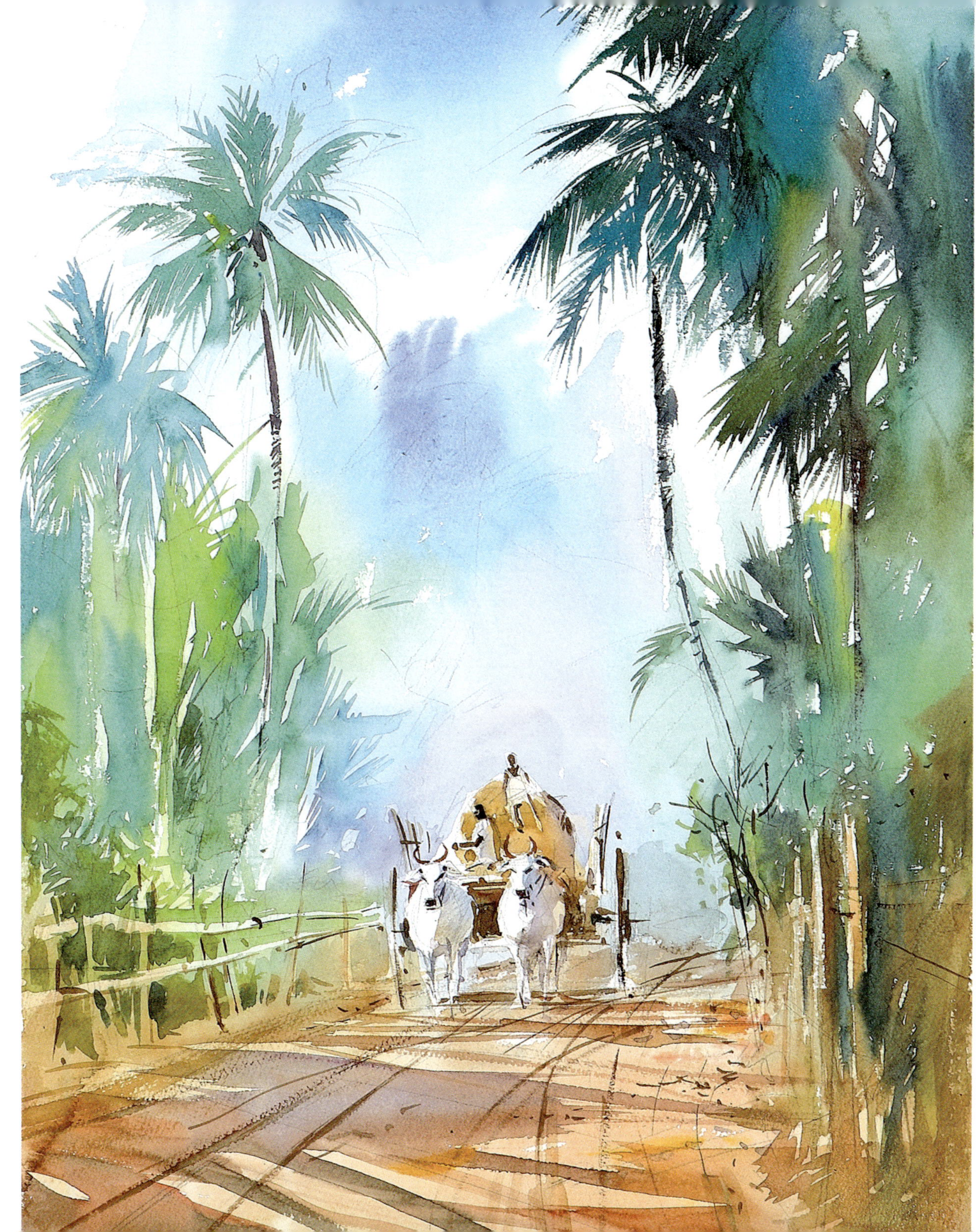

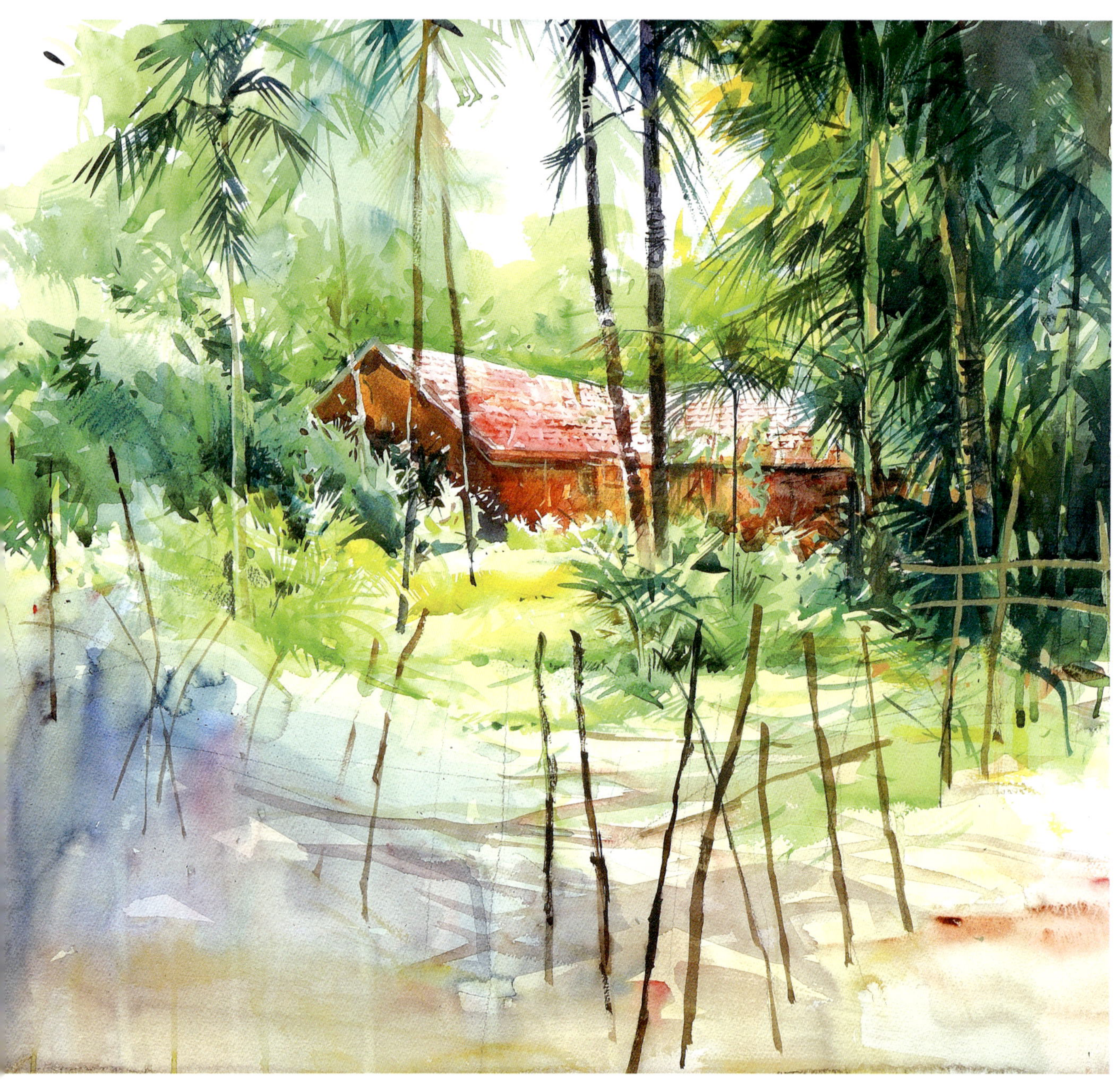

Assignment Seven

Try these examples for practice of brushwork. But that is not enough. You will find many subjects around you. Try painting these with suggestive as well as positive calligraphic brushstrokes.

Practice of brushwork is not only practice for your hands, it is an exercise in developing your skills of observation too. It is your observations that you are putting down on paper with the help of the brush.

Once we master our brushwork, we can make a painting out of just a few vertical and horizontal strokes. In both these paintings, the initial washes were applied with abandon.

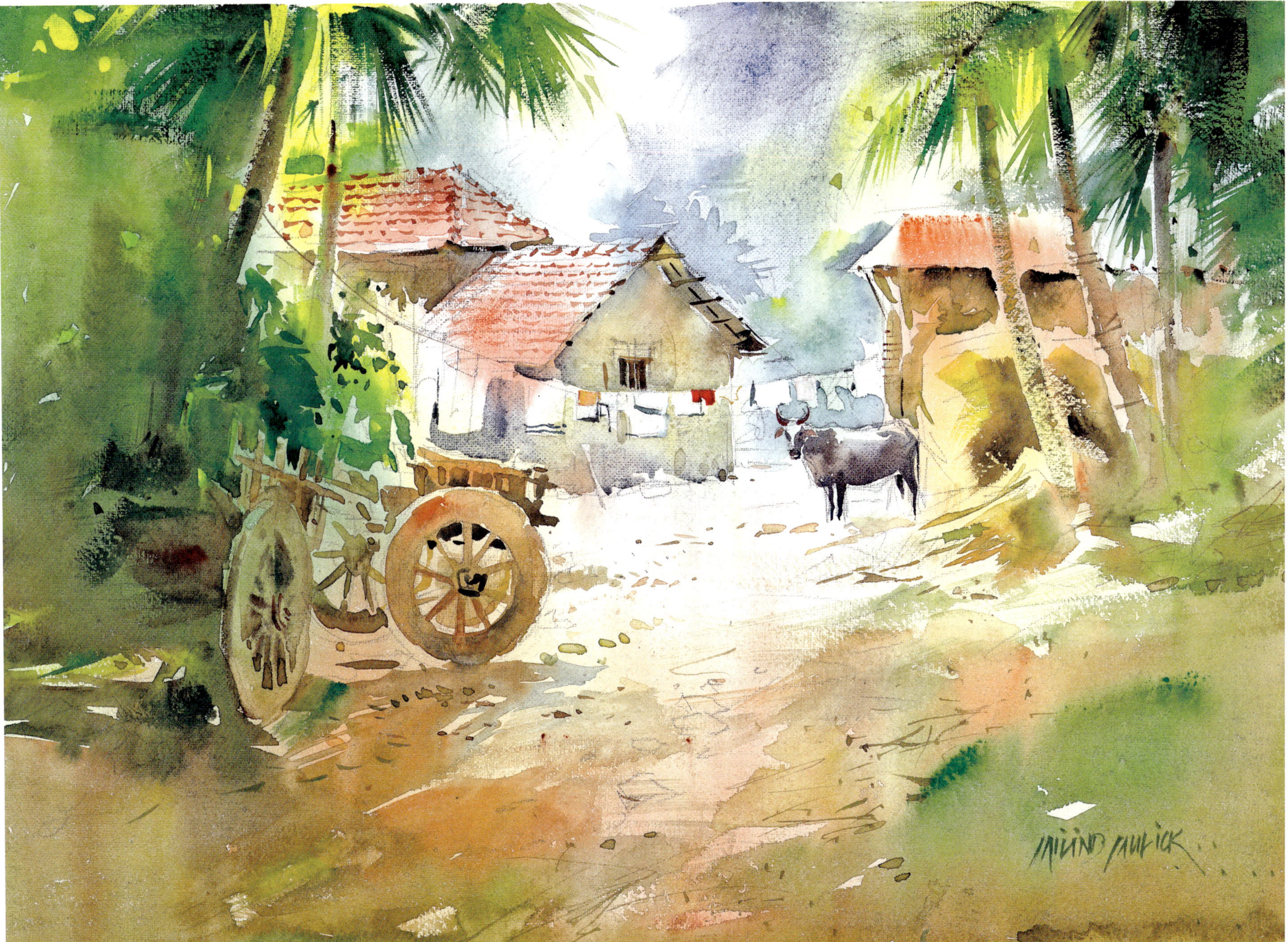
MILIND MULLICK

Subtraction

There is some similarity between painting a watercolour and sculpting from a block of stone. A sculpture can be made in two ways. One is to 'add' clay or Plaster of Paris and build up the sculpture step by step. On the other hand, when sculpting from stone or similar material we chip off progressively till we get the final stage. To put it differently we finish the sculpture by 'subtracting' from the original block.

To extend this analogy, when we paint we 'subtract' the white of the paper. Often, the centre of attraction of a painting is a white space or light area 'left out' while painting darker tones around it. Thus, it is defined by what is around it. So, what is left out becomes more important than what is painted.

To understand this further, let us go back to the bullock-cart in the previous painting. The first thing that catches our eye is the patches of sunlight on the bullocks' backs. Yet, these areas are the unpainted ones. Similarly the patches of sunlight on the road attract our attention because of the dark strokes of the shadows around them. This then is the message – In a watercolour, the unpainted areas are as important (in fact more) as the painted areas.

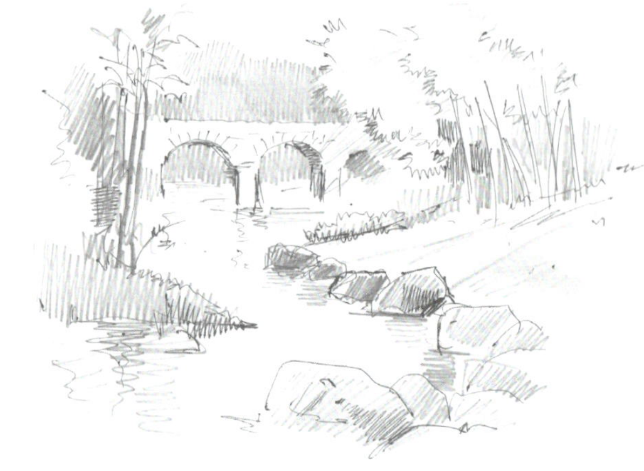

Generally when we set out to paint we are thinking about what we are going to paint. But, without our being fully aware of it, our brush strokes are defining the unpainted areas too. The painted areas are called 'positive' whereas the unpainted areas are termed the 'negative' spaces.

To understand this better, look at the letters WATERCOLOUR alongside. Consider the unpainted portion as 'positive', rather than the painted one. Try out this exercise with some different word.

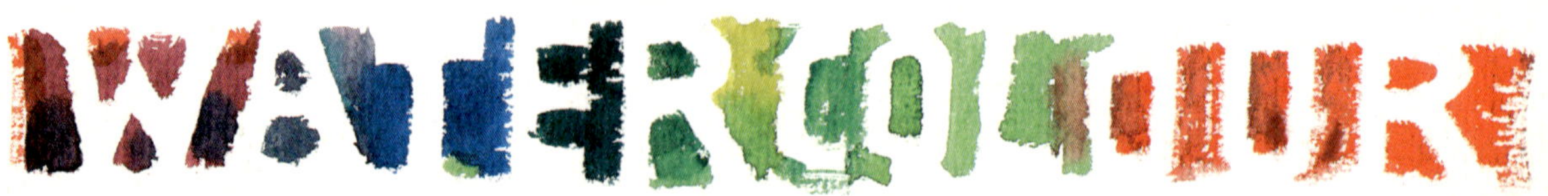

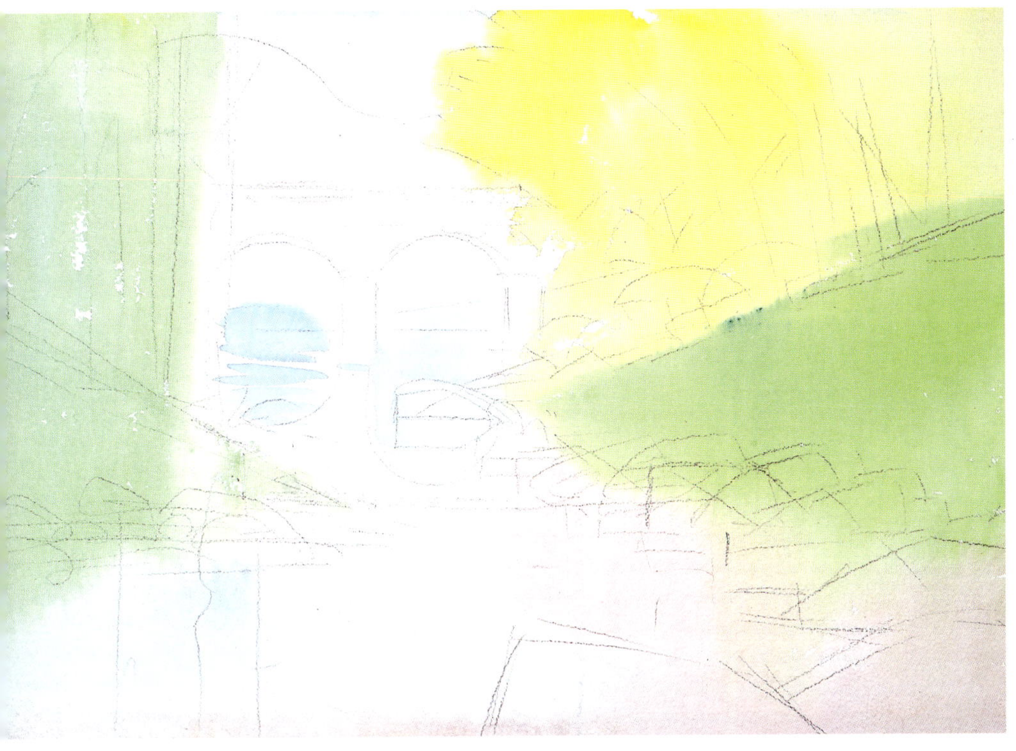

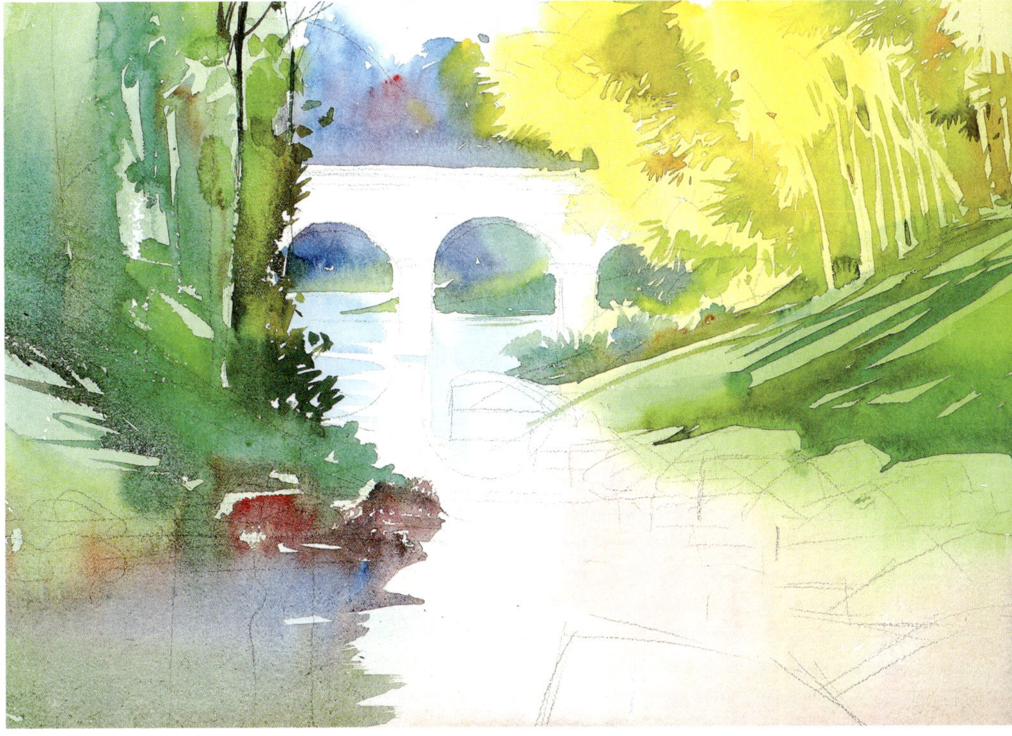

Let us try the subtraction technique with the help of this demonstration:

The sketch shows a stream with a small bridge across it. There are shrubs all around with a bamboo clump to the right. A few rocks are scattered in the water and along the banks.

I first applied a wash of yellow for the bamboo and yellow-green along with some shades of green for the foliage. Simultaneously I used blue-violet for the water and rocks. I took care to keep the bridge unpainted.

Now look carefully at the second stage. I have used blue for the sky and green with dark Prussian blue in such a way that the yellow bamboo and the leaves have suddenly become more prominent. Similarly a few strokes of orange and sap green have brought out the details of the bamboo clump. The space between the trunks have been painted dark so that the bamboo clumps stand out. Note that the dark tones do not attract our attention as much as the underlying yellow that was left out. While painting the rocks in dark blue and violet I have left the glistening highlights unpainted.

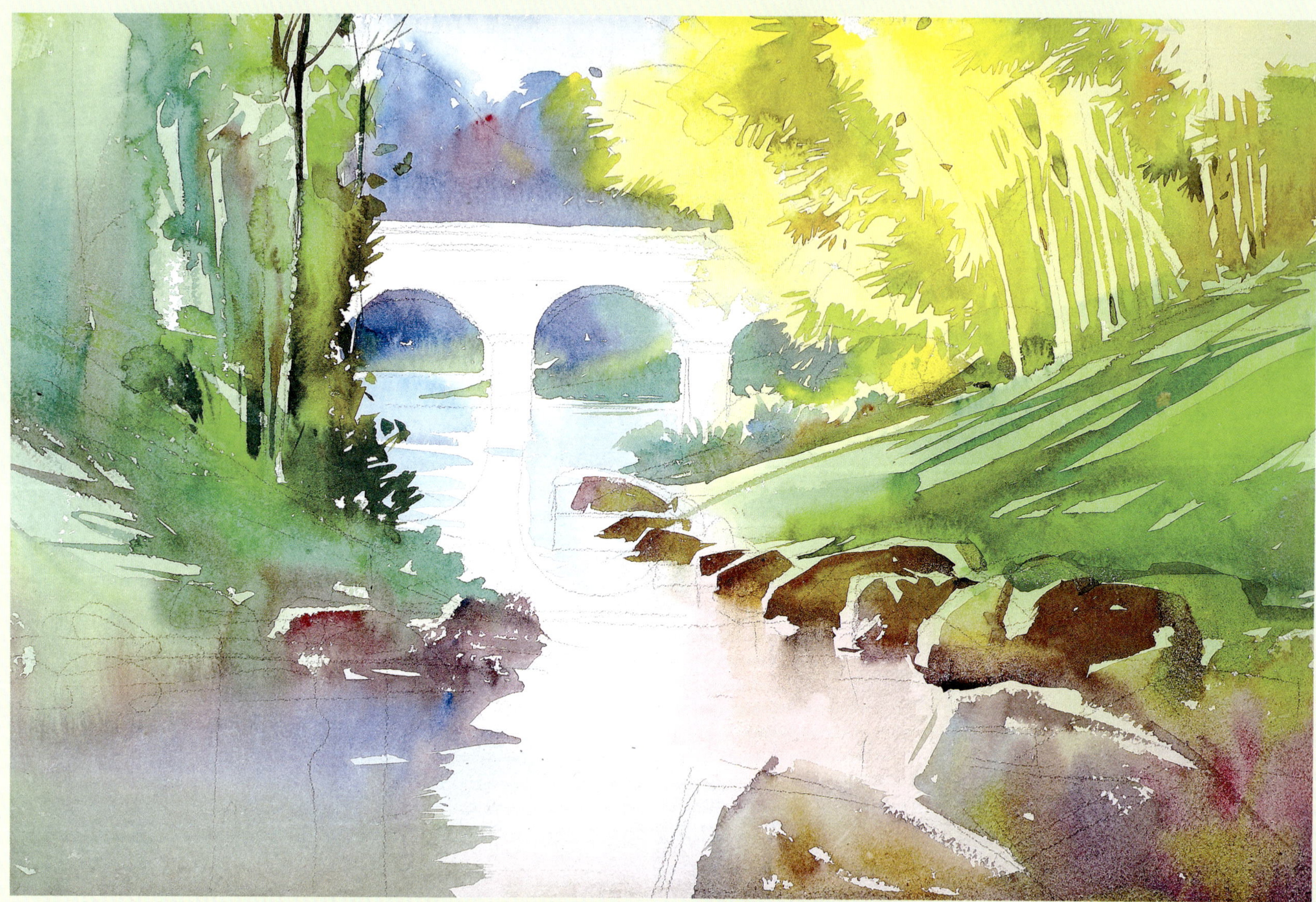

In the third step I have painted yellow, green, and blue patches in the water, excluding the reflections of the bridge. The shadows on the banks have been rendered with dark green strokes. The final stage reveals how the 'real' picture has emerged from the light, relatively 'unpainted' areas than the surrounding dark strokes.

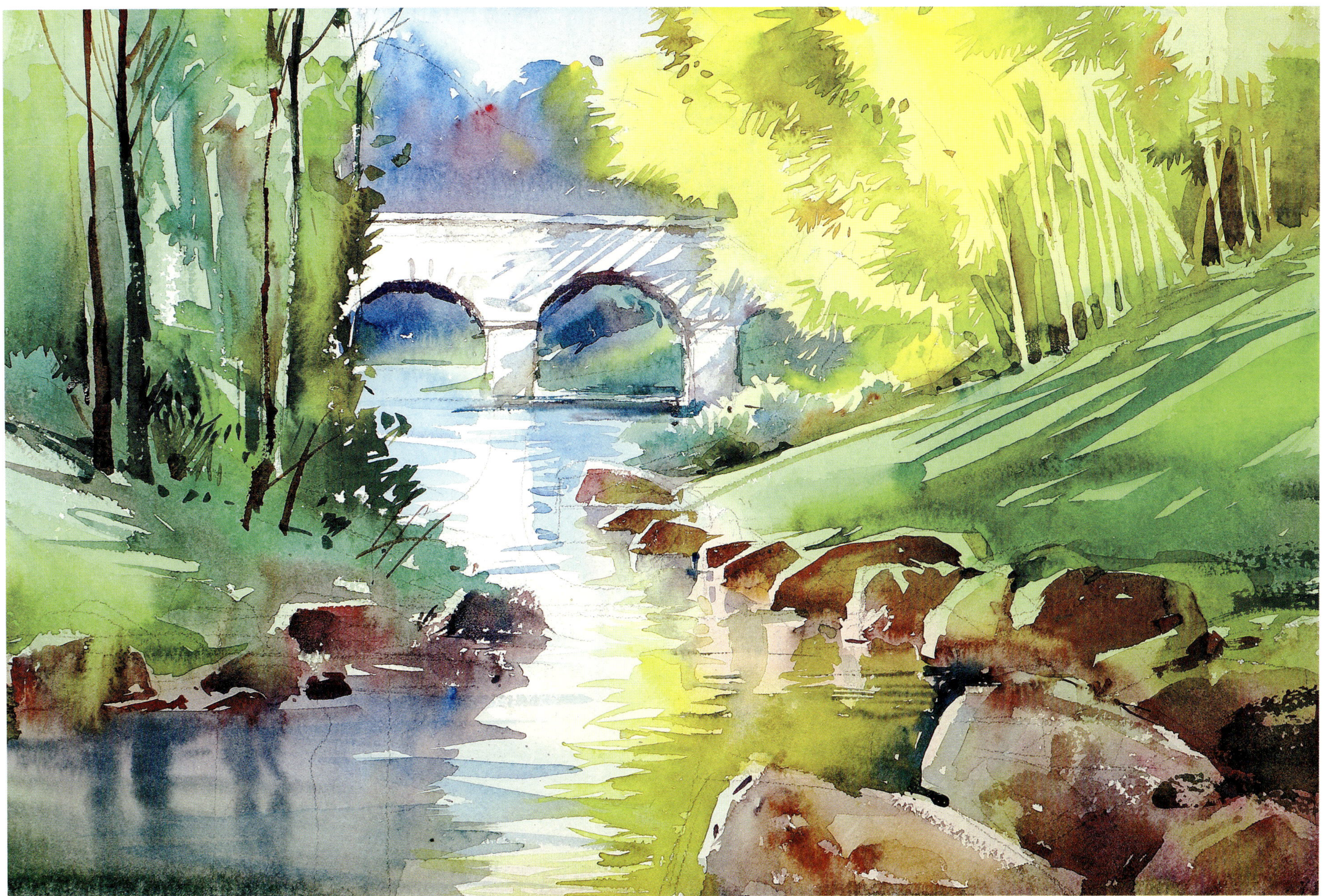

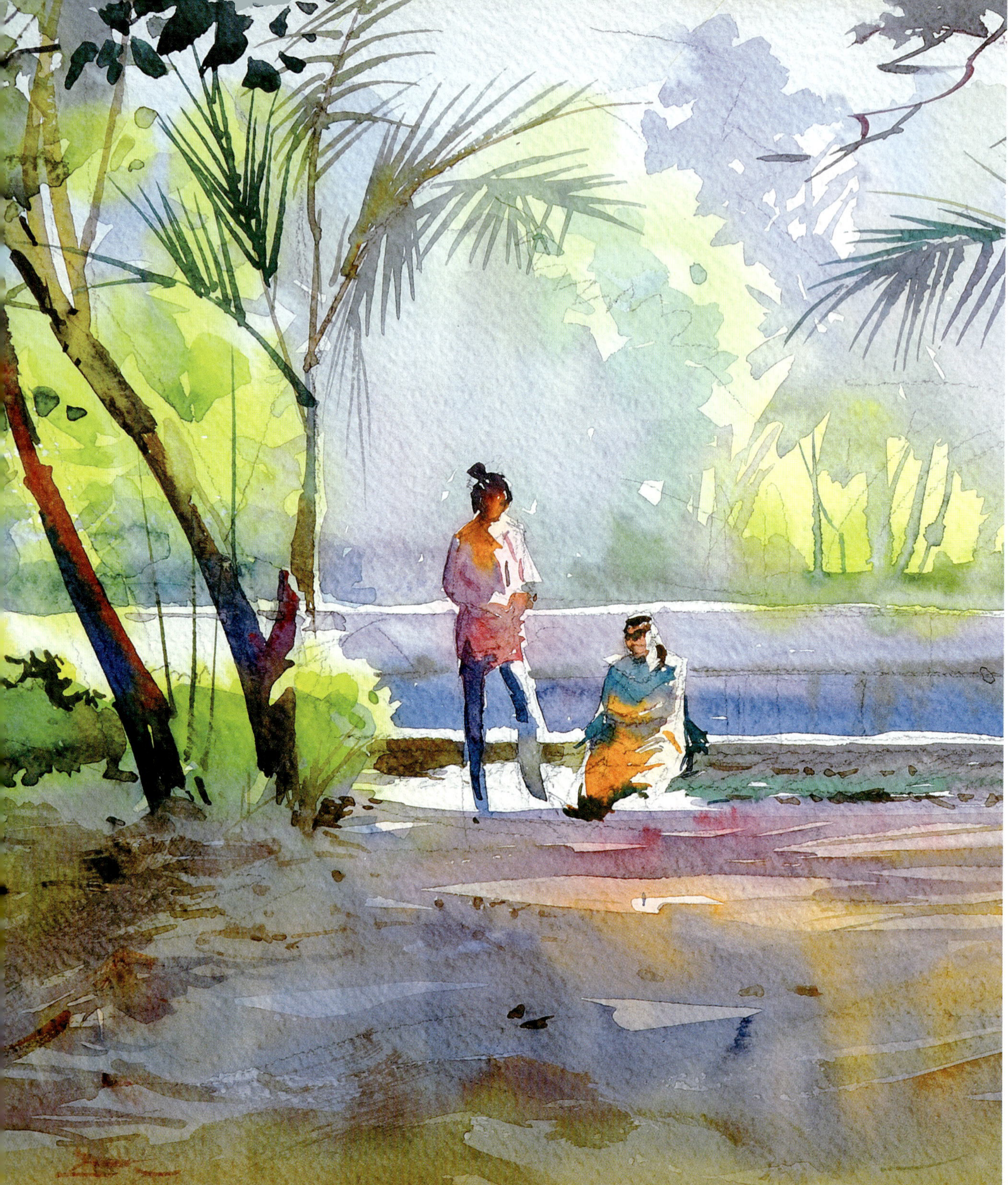

Assignment Eight

Understand the technique of subtraction by choosing subjects that have high contrast (dark-light). Keep a written record of the steps you used in subtraction. This will help you to understand the process better.

Before you attempt a full painting, try small subjects such as a bunch of white flowers against a dark background or a white cup and saucer in bright sunlight and so on.

White represents light. Watercolours are transparent. White paint is never used in a watercolour painting. 'White' in a watercolour is the area we leave unpainted, wherever we desire.

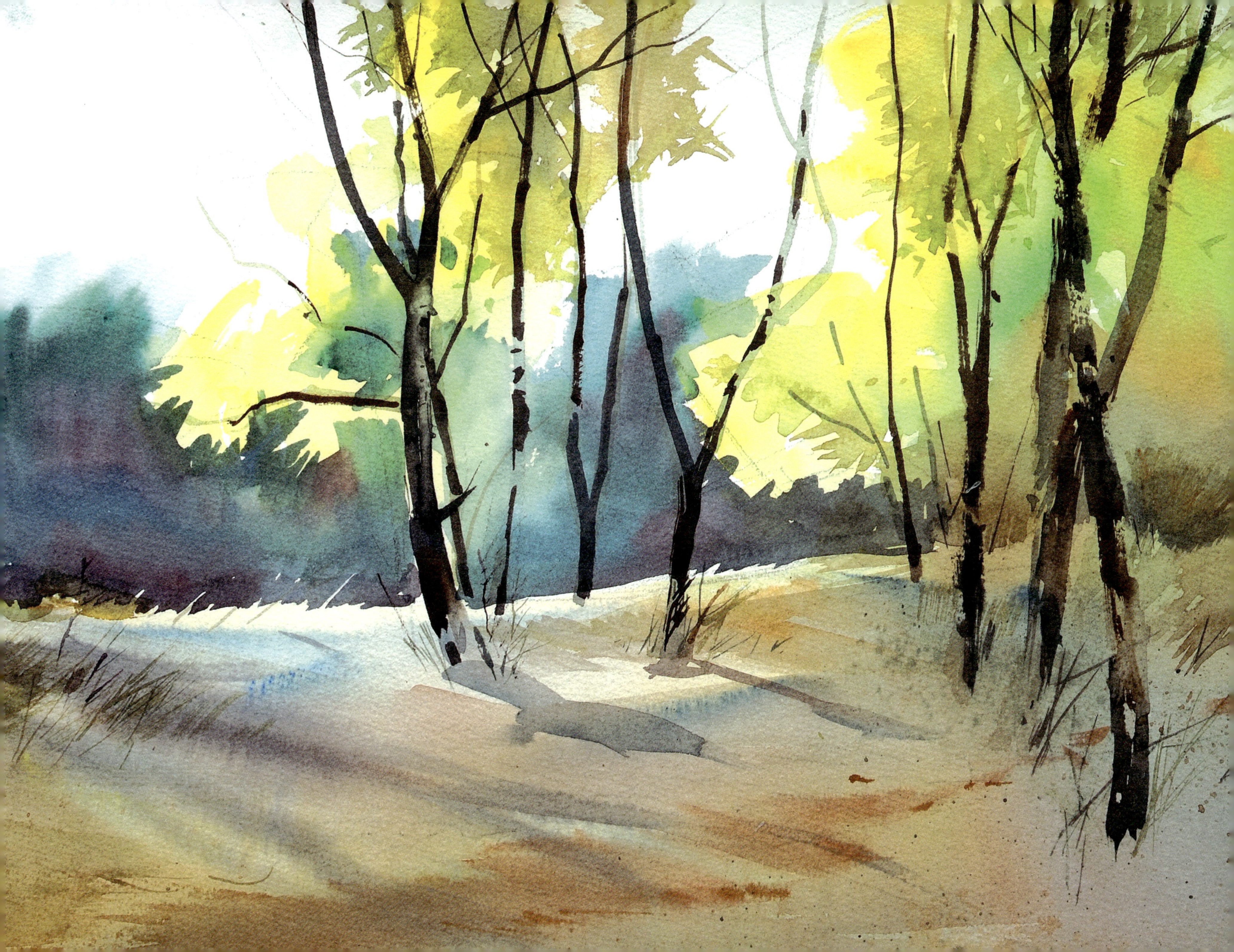

Lesson Nine

All in One

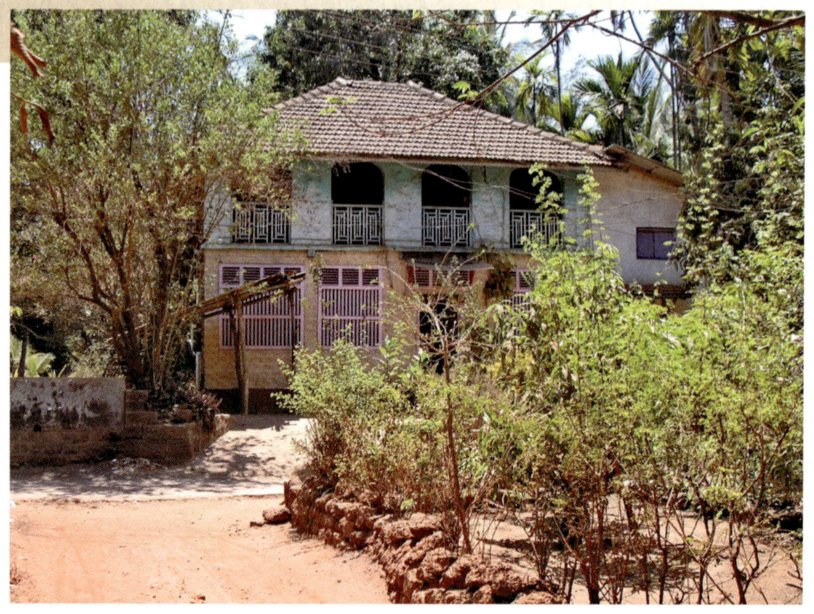

Here we are going to revise all the techniques that we have learnt so far. Though we have learnt them individually, we will be using them together for this exercise.

Here, a photograph will be used as reference. Further in the book, in Lesson Twelve, we shall see in detail, how to use a photograph while painting.

In any photograph, there are many forms and shapes. The first step is to break these up into six or seven shapes of different sizes. In other words, we are simplifying the picture or the scene in front of us. This makes the painting much simpler than what we are faced with initially.

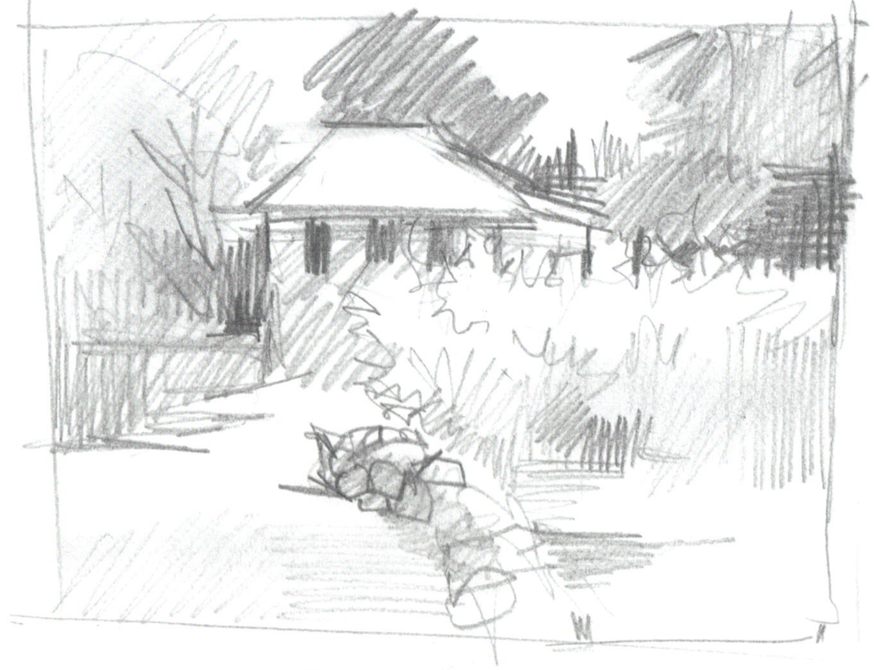

The colours / tones in the photograph have been applied in two simple shapes. I have painted directly without the clear cut steps of wash, glazing or wet-in-wet glazing.

The foliage in front of the house has been done in lemon yellow and a bit of sap green. The bright sunlight on the trees will be done later. To the left of the house I have used lemon yellow, sap green and a bit of orange. But for the background trees and to the right of the house I wanted darker tones so I used Prussian blue and red along with green. For the approach road and stones I've used light orange since it was sunlit.

The photo shows the house in shade though its roof is bathed in sunlight. To show the shaded walls I have used vermilion / crimson to begin with and then viridian green for the upper parts. The sunlit foliage now stands out against the dark walls of the house (subtraction).

A little brown, red and blue were used to paint the shadows cast by the stones. This has defined their shapes. A few horizontal strokes across the foreground have further created the effect of a bright afternoon.

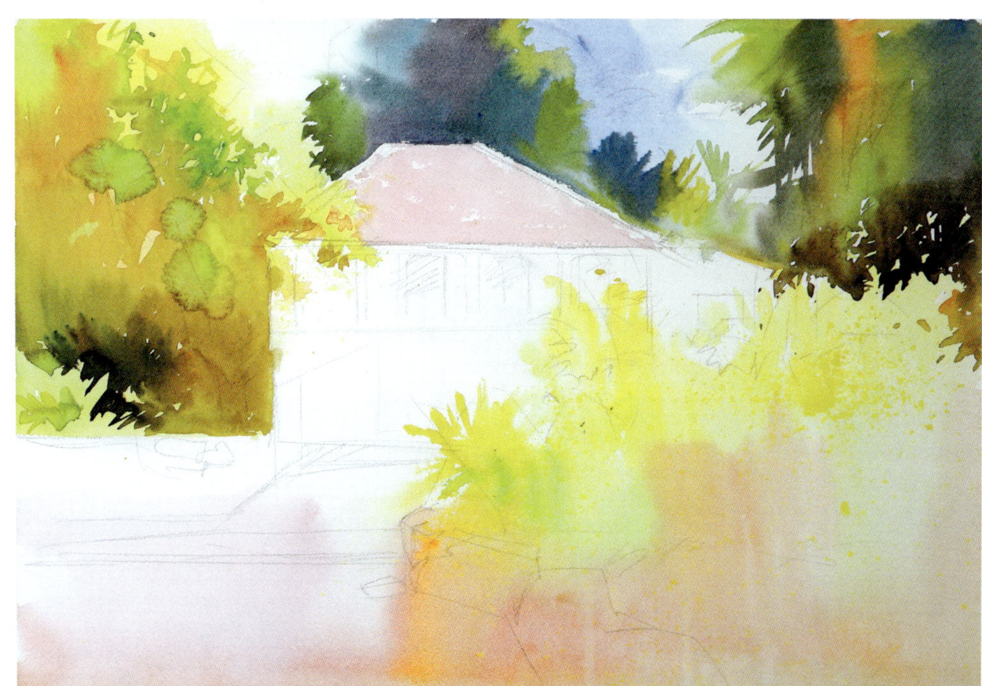

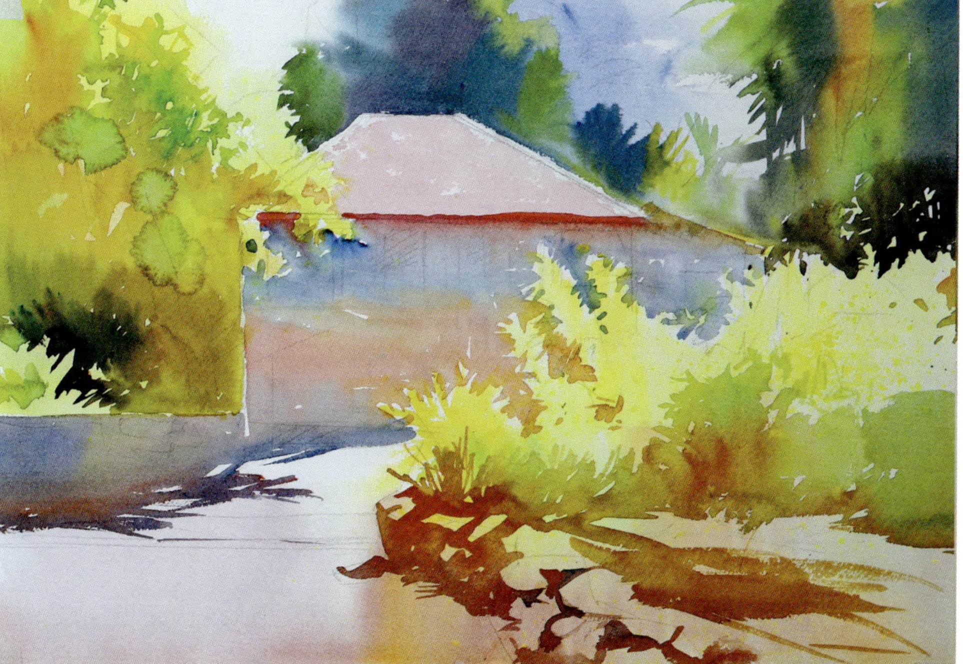

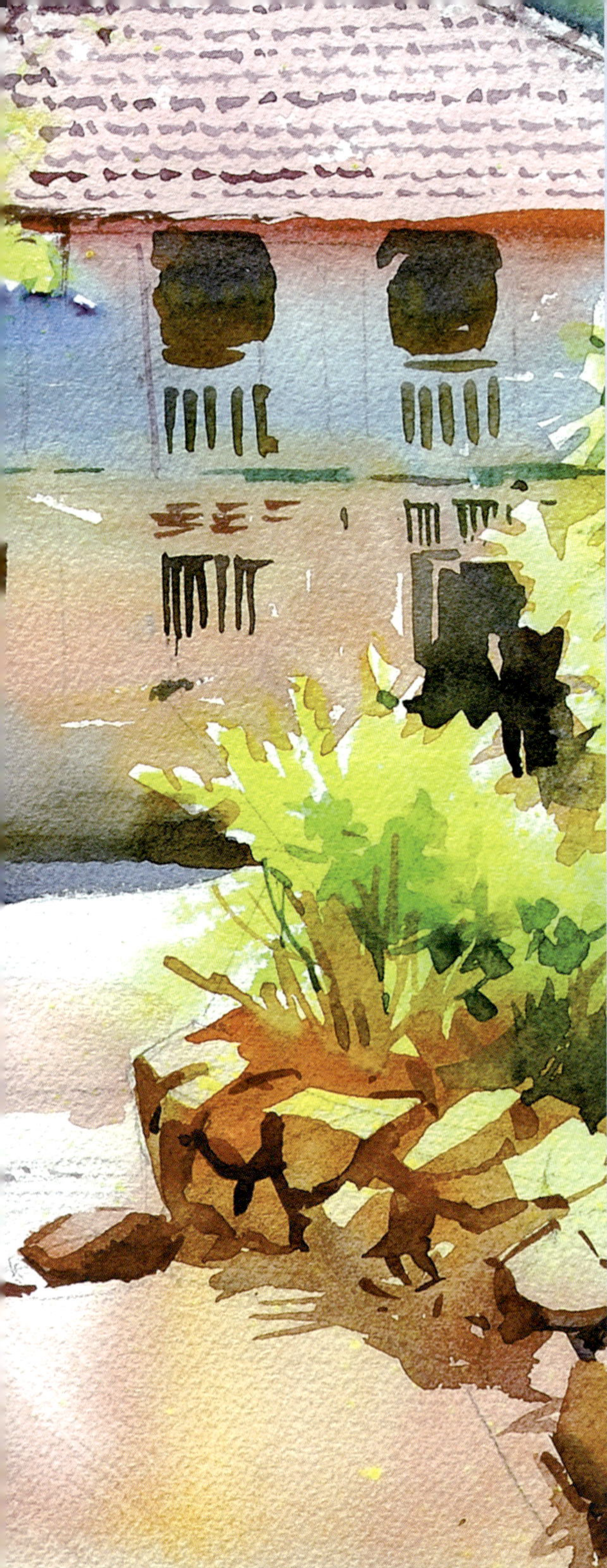

Pushing colours

It is an interesting fact that if we try to paint the exact colours as they appear to our eyes, the painting actually appears dull e.g. if we paint distant fields light green they appear as a flat patch of colour. The way out is to paint a few strokes using the colour adjacent (on the colour wheel) to the primary colour being used. So, when painting a field, you may apply some yellowish and bluish strokes along with the basic green and see how the result appears 'fresh'.

When painting shadows, it is not enough to mix black – in fact black is almost never used. This is because even in shadows we can see different colours. They are never black though they may appear so at first sight. Some light is reflected from the surrounding surfaces into the shadow areas. This reflected light adds some of its colour to the shadow. Similarly, in the shadow we see the 'opposite' colour of the basic colour e.g. the shadow of a red surface contains green (which appears opposite red on the colour wheel), or the shadow of a yellow surface has some violet in it. If we employ these facts while choosing our colours we will find our paintings getting more realistic.

Assignment Nine

Try to understand each step carefully while copying this demonstration. We get large areas by giving washes. Wet-in-wet gives us tonal variations. Glazing helps us to build up shapes and tones. Brushwork binds all these together. While doing all this we are also employing 'subtraction'. Choose a suitable photograph and using the above steps, try to make a painting, using the photograph as reference.

Once the paper had dried I showed the doors and windows with a few strategic vertical strokes in dark tones without any detailing.

Similarly in the surrounding foliage I painted in some branches with a pointed brush. Note how the painting appears complete and realistic though no details have been painted.

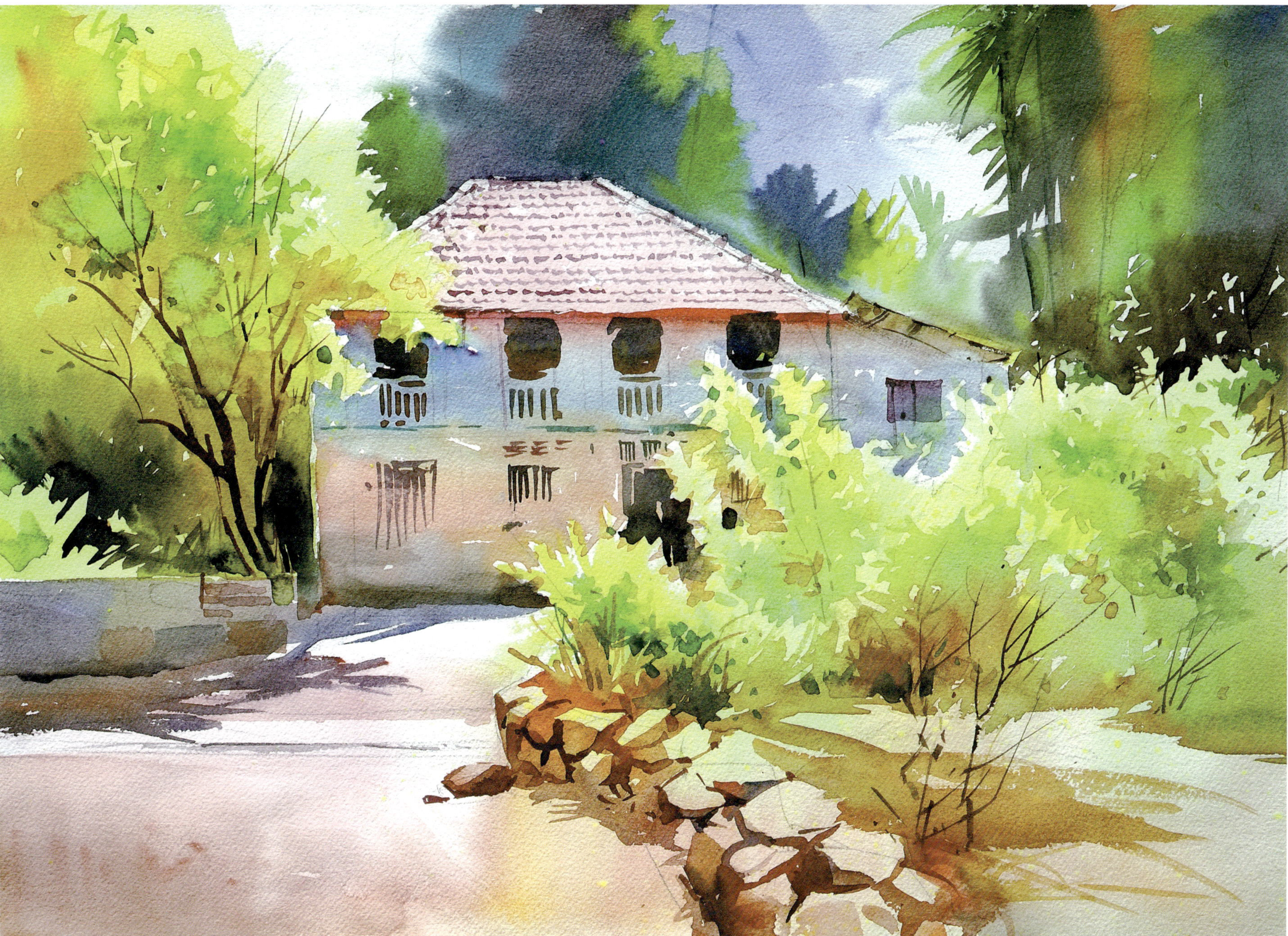

Direct Approach

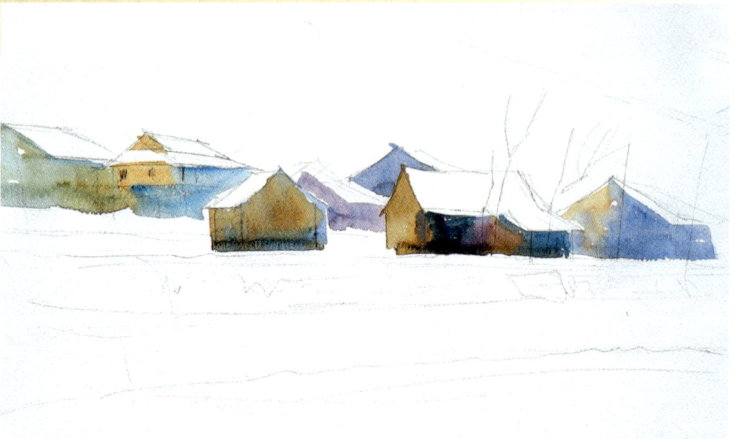

Thus far we have studied washes, glazing and brushwork in a somewhat compartmentalized manner. But in this painting I have worked by filling out the appropriate tones in the respective areas as I saw them before my eyes. In other words, I painted without being consciously aware of the techniques we have seen so far. This may thus be termed the 'direct' method.

First I used orange, burnt sienna and crimson (warm) and cobalt blue (cool) together to paint the walls, leaving the roofs untouched. The warm colours suggest light whereas the cool colours give a hint of shaded area.

Next, the mountain slope was done in a single flowing wash using more or less cool colours. The white unpainted portion creates the effect of snow on the mountain and on the roofs.

In the third step I have given a greenish wash for the foreground, leaving the right corner unpainted into which I applied a light blue wash. Most of this painting was over now. The few final strokes of dark green and reddish blue have given the effect of the sloping mountain and have added depth to the painting.

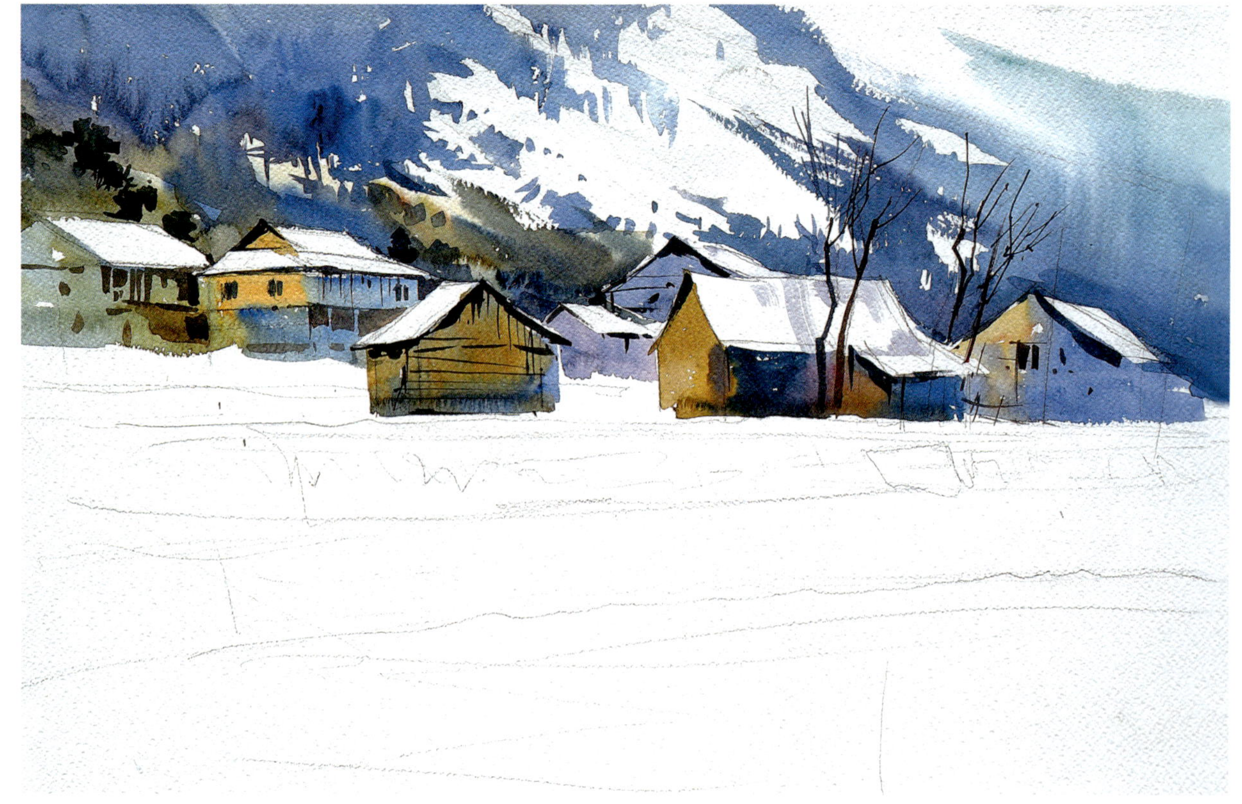

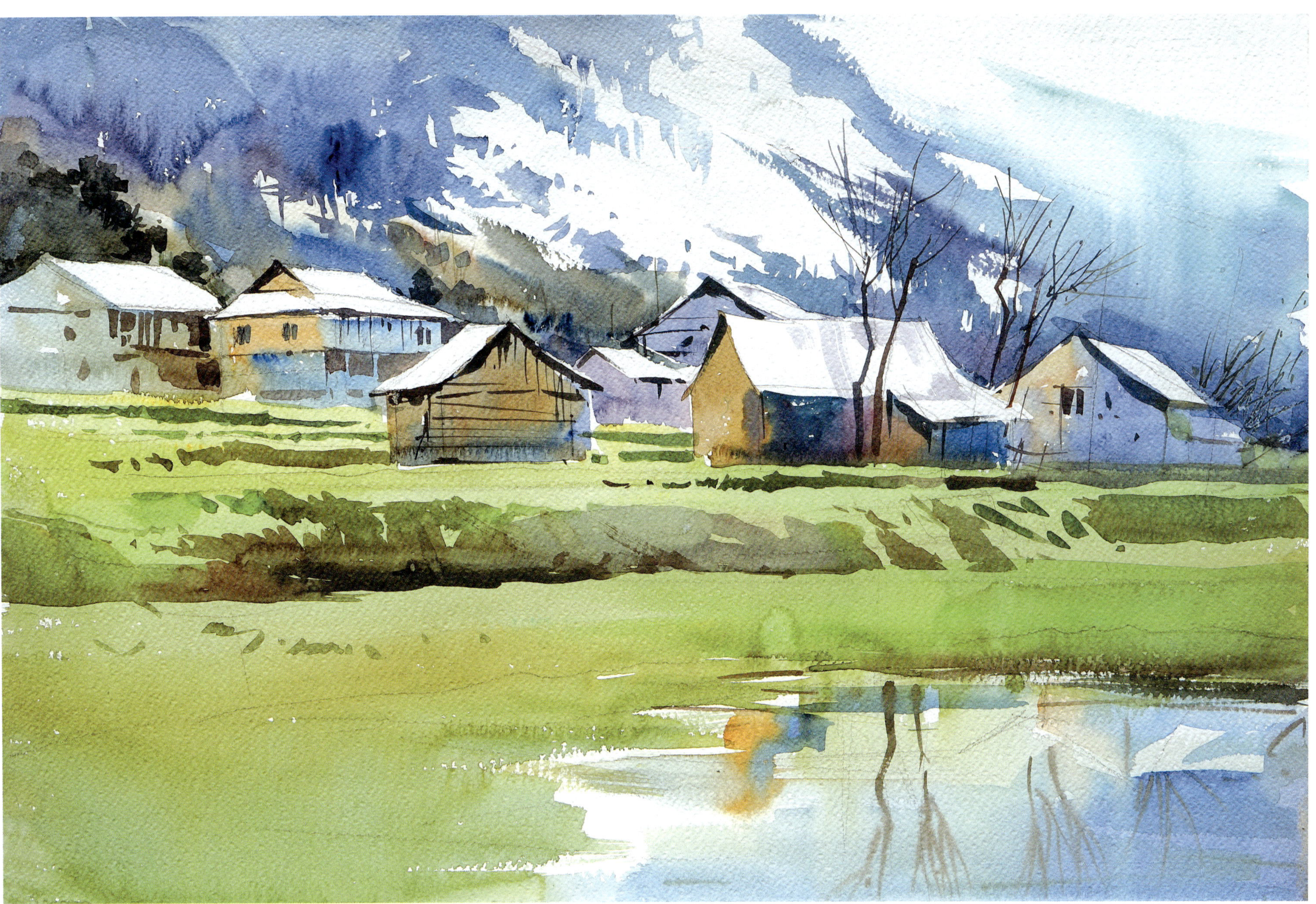

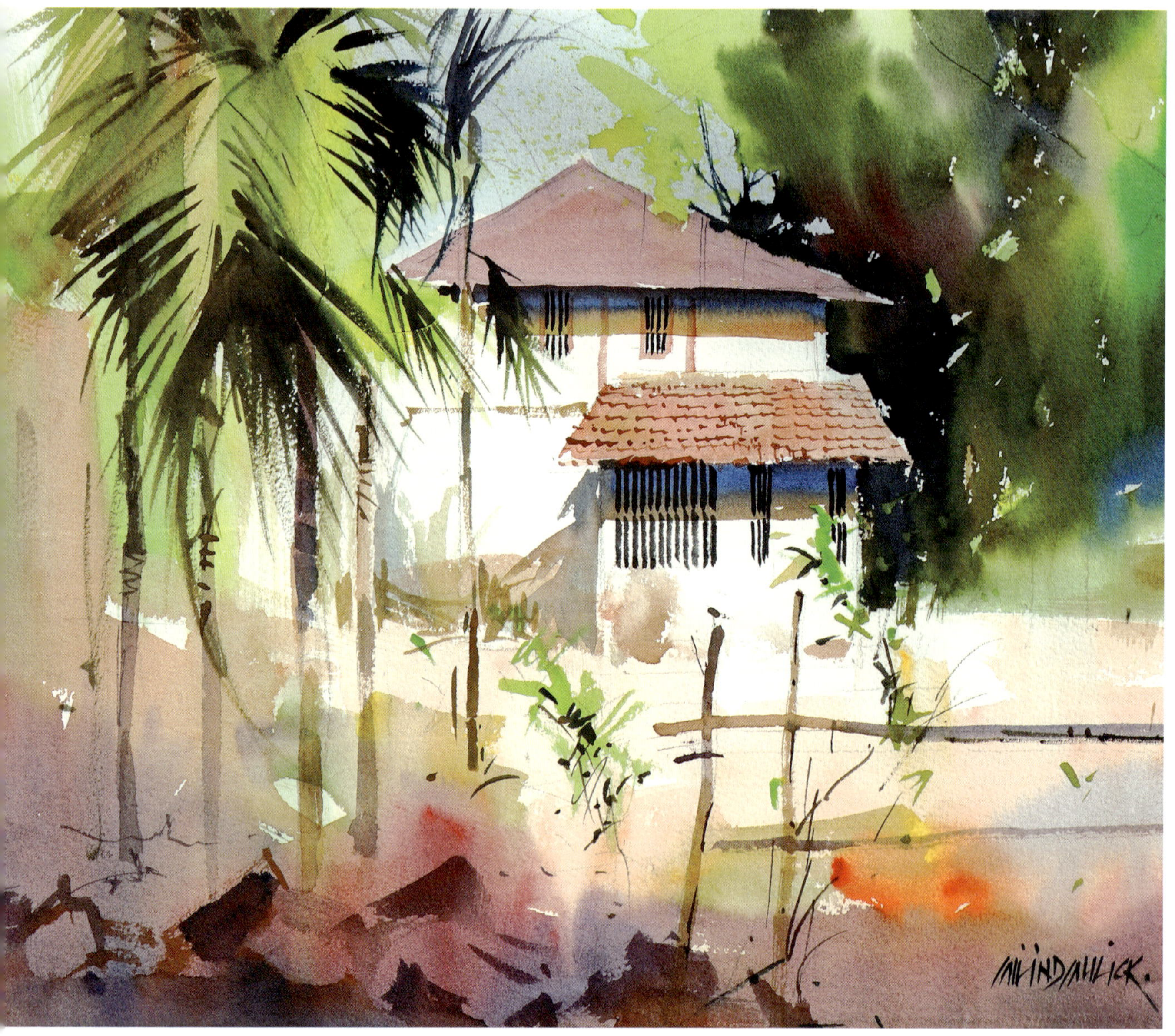

Assignment Ten

When you are practising the direct approach, try and make your work more expressive. If you think up some unusual colour, do not hesitate to put it down. Be bold in your brushwork!

When composing a painting we have to think of the elements as well as the colours. In this painting, the red in the shade has balanced the red roof. Overall, the reds and greens have balanced each other and hold the painting together. The two horizontal strokes for the fence balance the vertical lines of the windows and the tree trunks.

At first glance, the scene for the painting on the right may appear uninteresting. But the subject arouses interest because of the play of sunlight and shadows, as well as the different colours in the foliage. Here too, the vertical tree trunks are balanced by the horizontal strokes of the shadows.

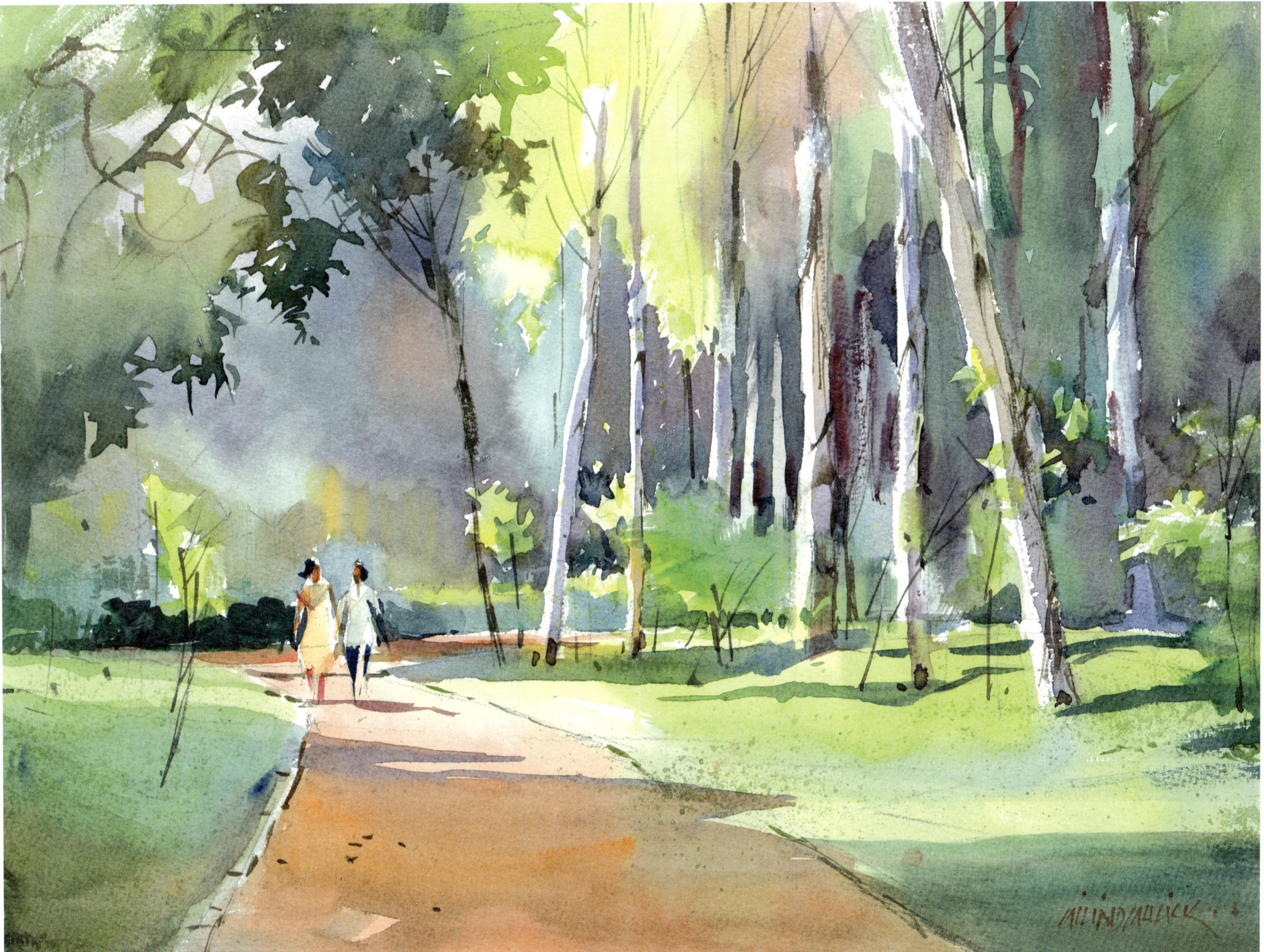
MILIND MULLICK

Lesson Eleven

Outdoors

When working outdoors our equipment needs to be compact and portable. An aluminium folding stand and a folding stool are convenient to carry.

Initially one hesitates to paint outdoors. To get over this bashfulness it helps to form a group of like-minded enthusiasts.

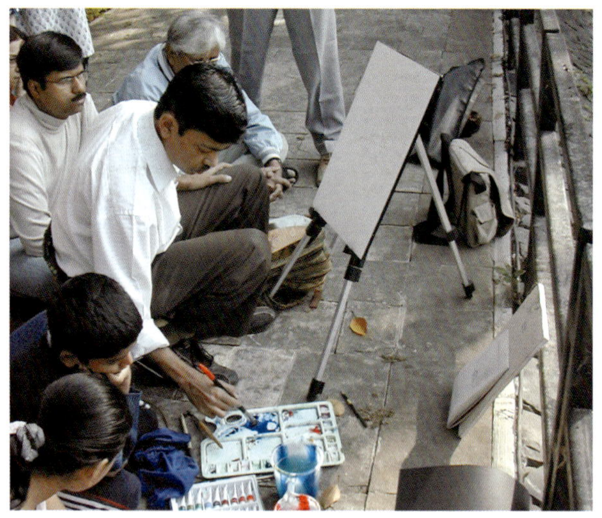

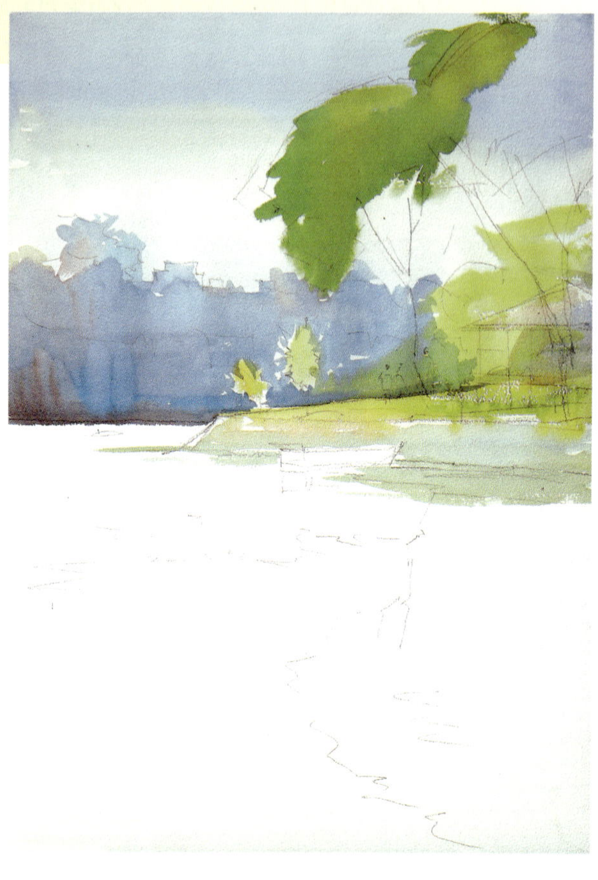

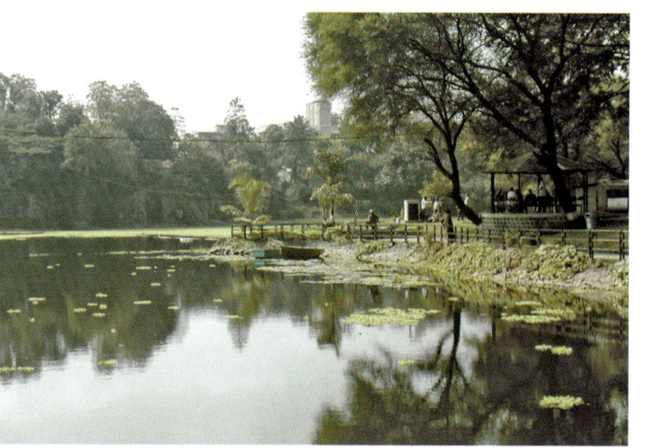

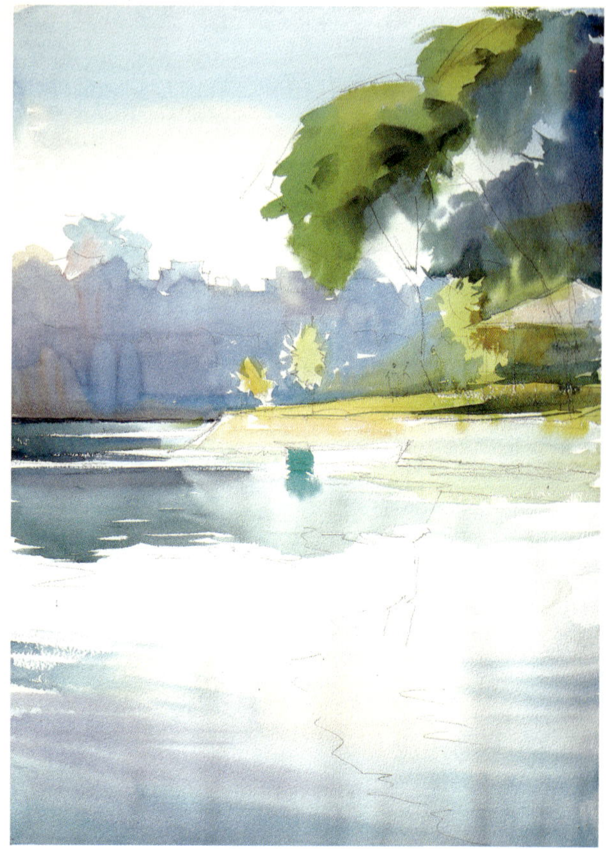

When faced with a complex scene while painting outdoors we are often vexed by the question 'what to paint?' There seem to be simply too many things!

If you look at the photograph alongside you will see many pictures 'hidden' in it. I chose the tree, the shade beneath it, the boat and the reflections of all these in the lake.

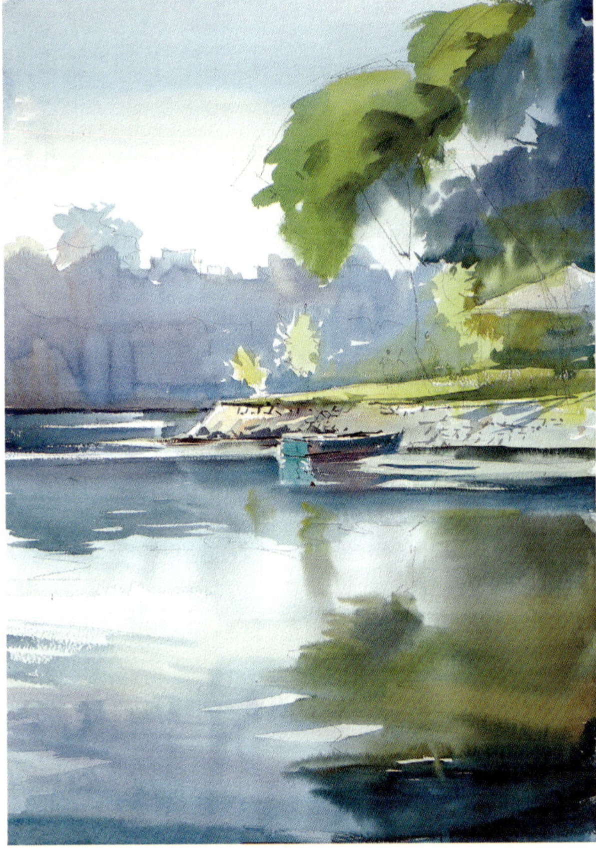

First I painted in what I felt were the main elements with a grey wash. This is very important – knowing what to choose from the many elements in front of us.

Remember that we have cameras to capture the little details. That is not the job of the artist.

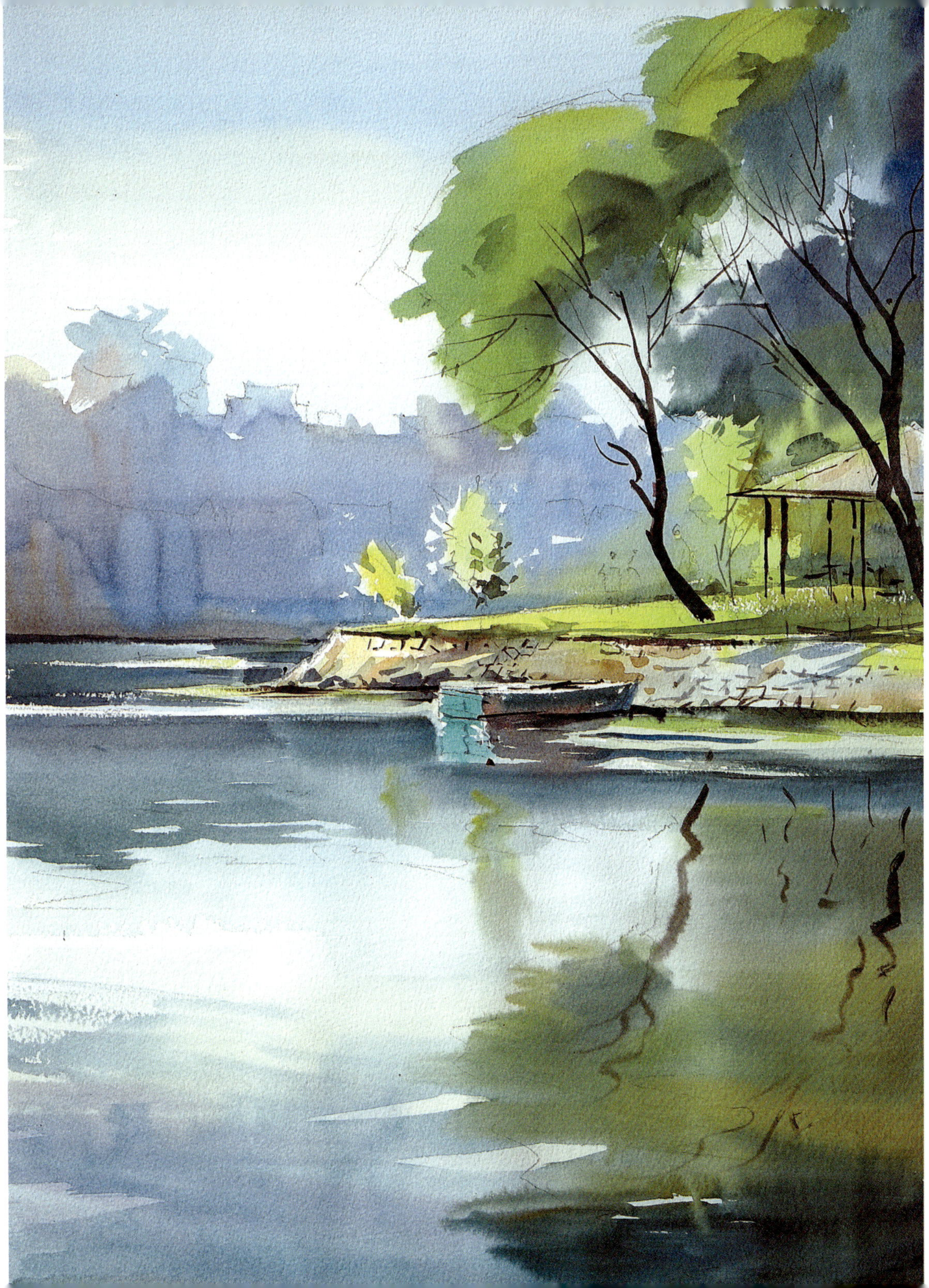

While sketching or painting outdoors, we tend to first draw or paint the forms or areas that have appealed the most to us. Then we fill in the other details. We are then faced with the question of when to stop this process. However, practice teaches us as we go along. Slowly each of us develops a unique way of choosing the essential elements from the scene. It is precisely for this reason that every painting is different from a photograph.

Once you are sufficiently experienced in painting on the spot, it is alright to use photographs for reference.

Assignment Eleven

There is no alternative to painting on the spot. Try painting the same spot at different times. You will see how the ambient light affects the outcome.

Similarly, study painting the same spot but with different compositions.

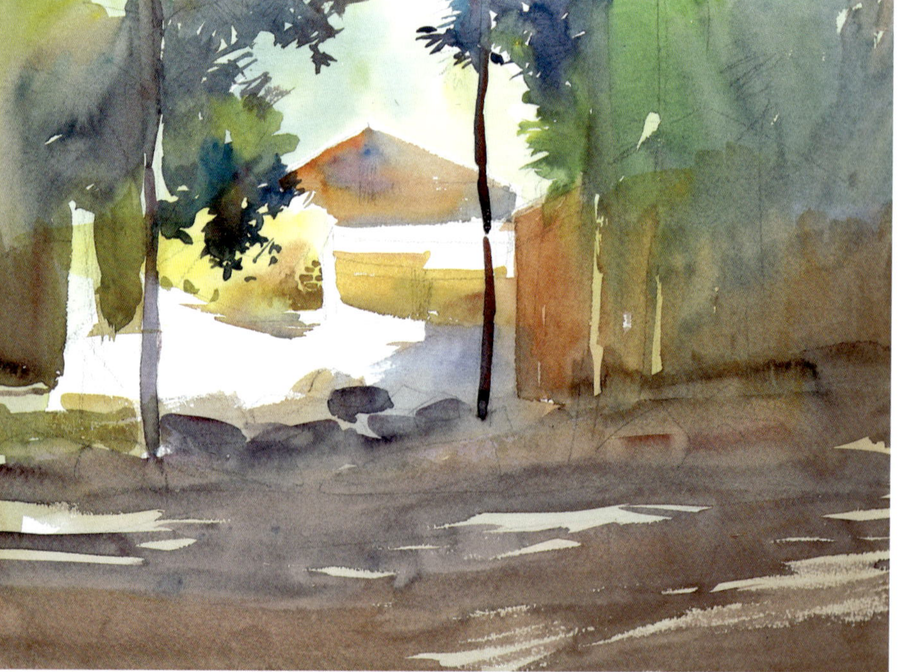

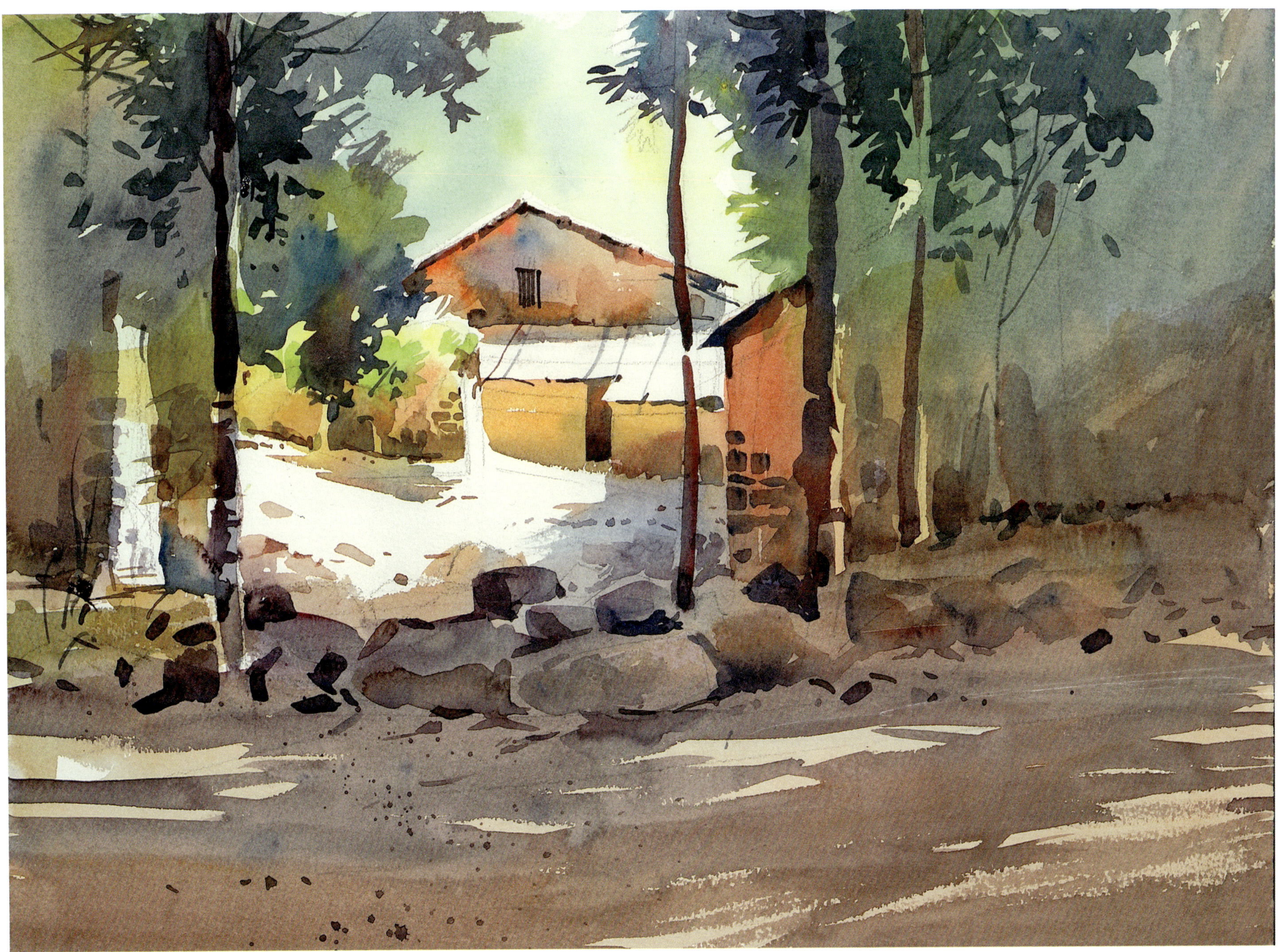

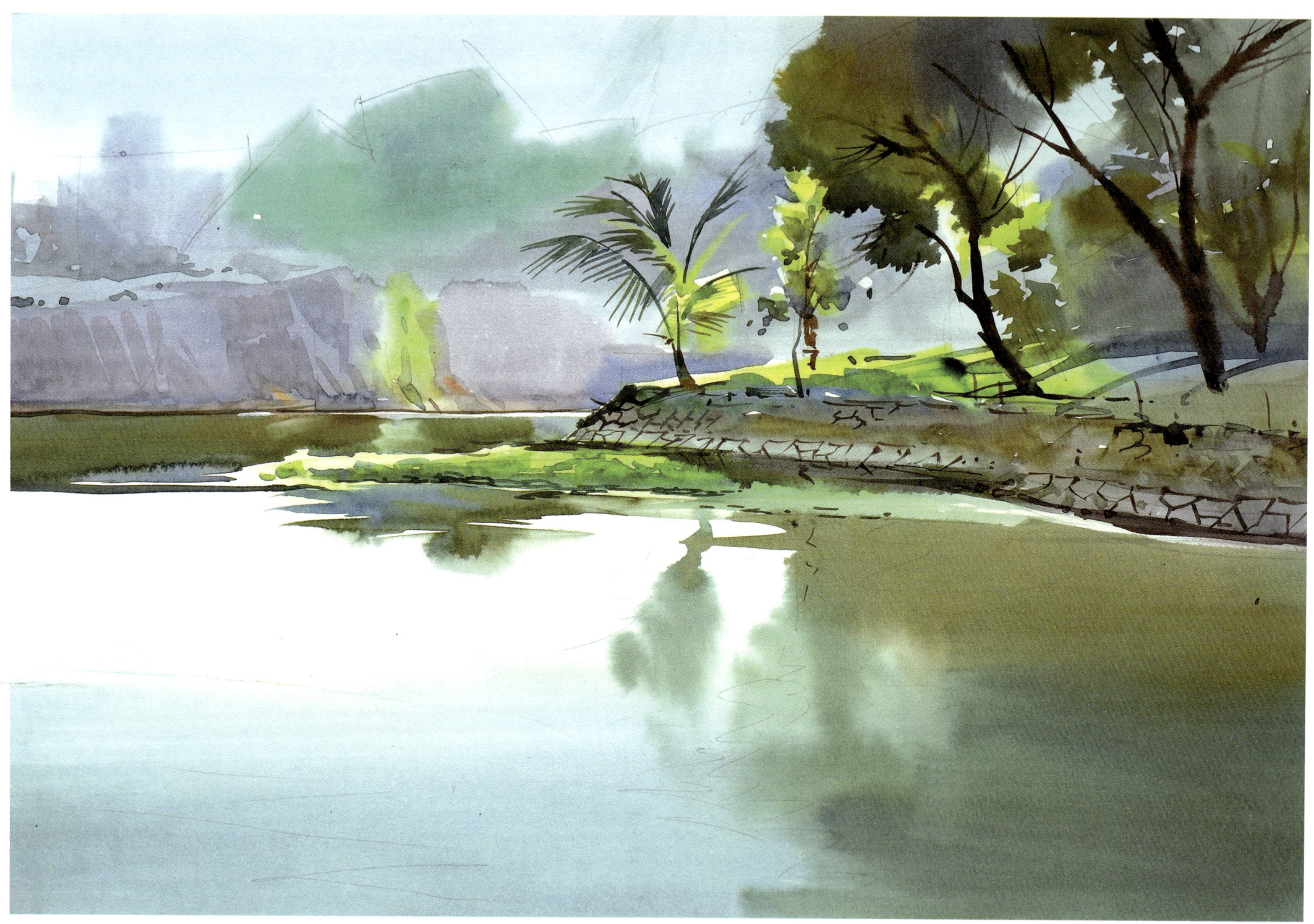

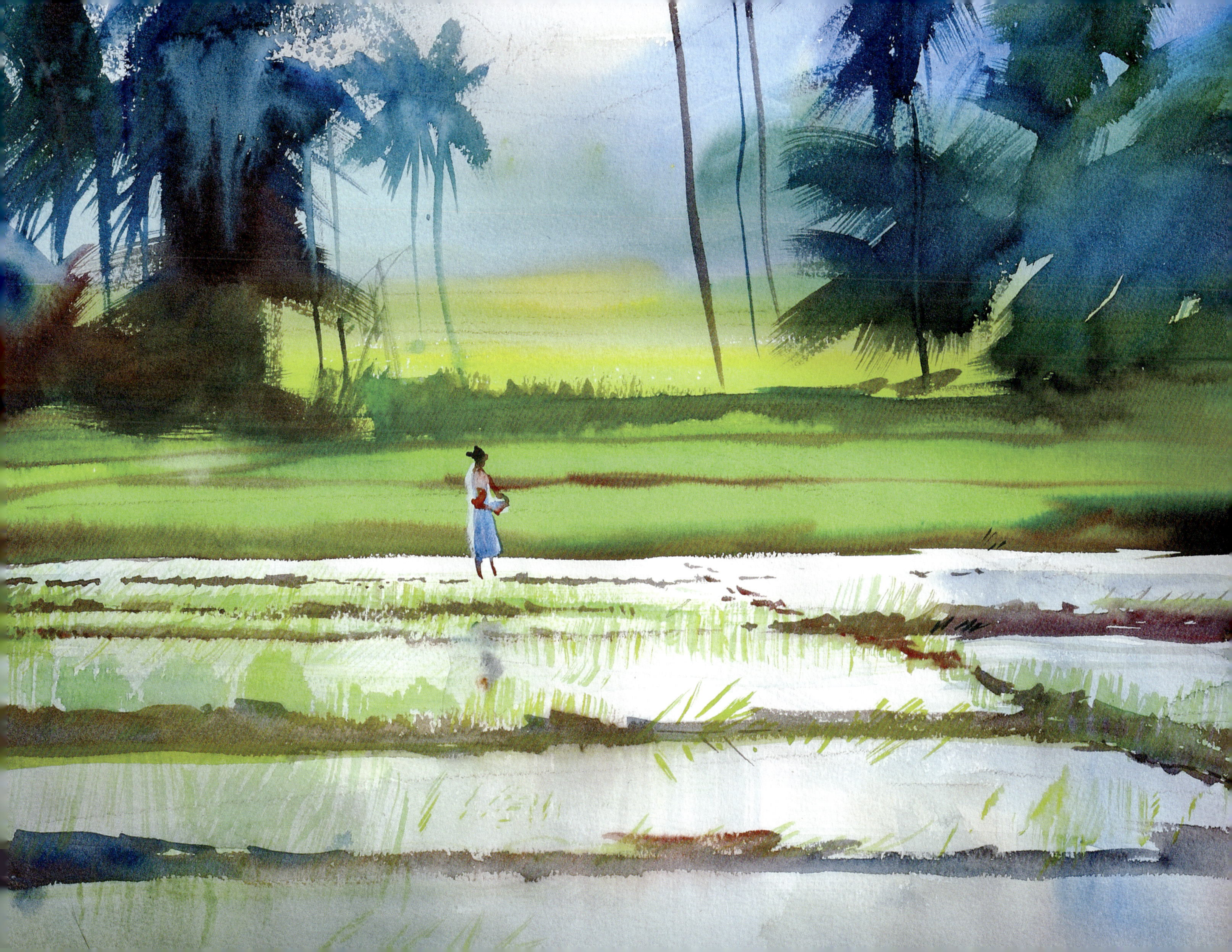

Reference Photographs

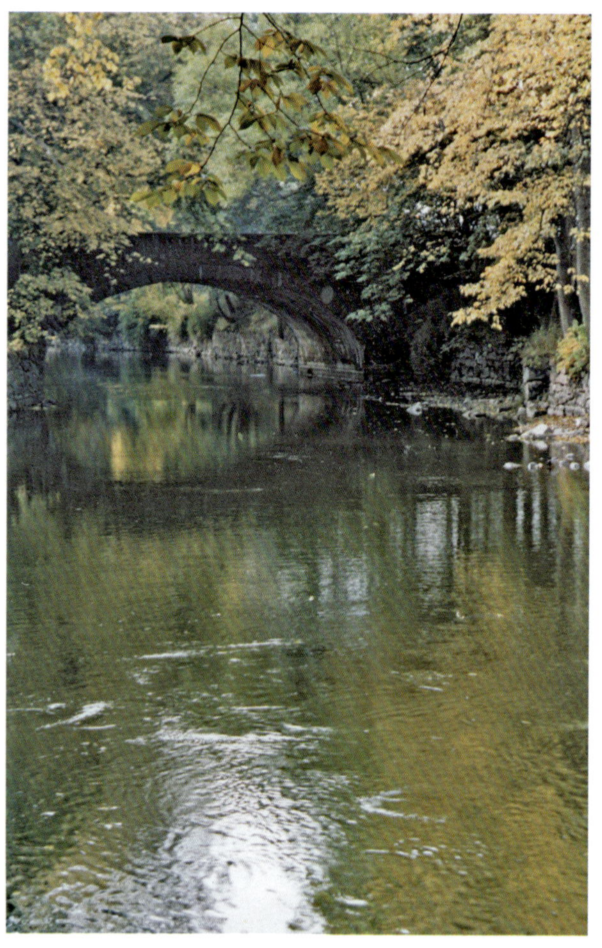

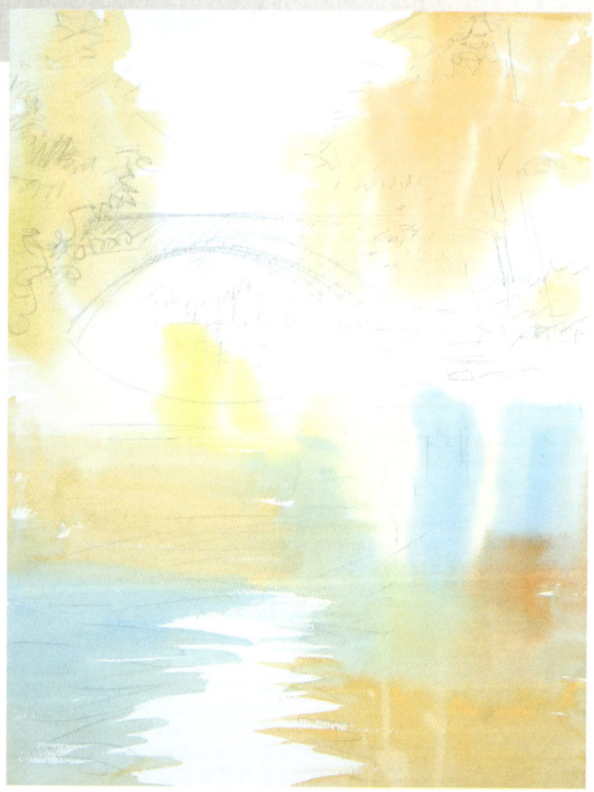

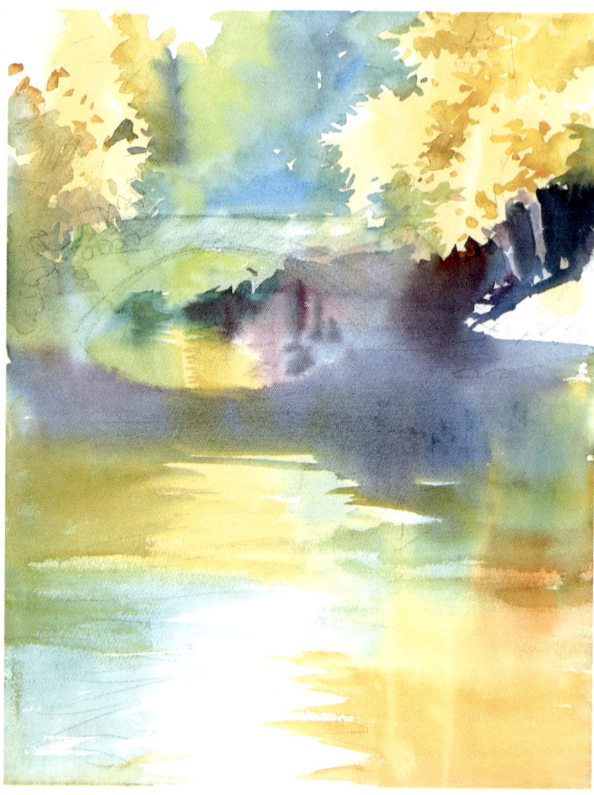

Whenever we look at any scene, the pupils of our eyes constantly adjust and give us a perception of the 'average' light. This happens although some areas are brightly lit, some are in shade and so on.

If we were to photograph a scene, the camera uses just one aperture that emphasizes the contrast – bright areas appear brighter and shadows appear darker than what they are. These limitations have to be kept in mind whenever a photograph is used as reference.

We are now going to paint from the photograph given alongside. The most important thing to remember is that we are not going to do a faithful, enlarged copy of the image. The photograph is only a reference. It is up to us to 'find' a painting in that photograph.

First of all I used chrome yellow for the trees and cerulean blue for the water and applied the required wash. In order to show some waves in the water, I took care to see that no sharp edges formed. While showing the blue-green distant foliage, I used 'subtraction' by painting around the yellow foreground so that the trees were brought out. Some dark tones were used to show the shadows in these trees.

Up to this stage light tones are dominant in this painting. Now the bridge and the portions above it have been done by glazing. The reflections in the water will be done by wet-in-wet glazing. The reflection of the bridge merges with the water. At the same time the sharp edges of the waves emphasize the bridge reflections.

In the final stages, dark violet has been used to paint the bridge walls along with some details. In this predominantly light-toned painting, the selective use of darks has generated the required contrast.

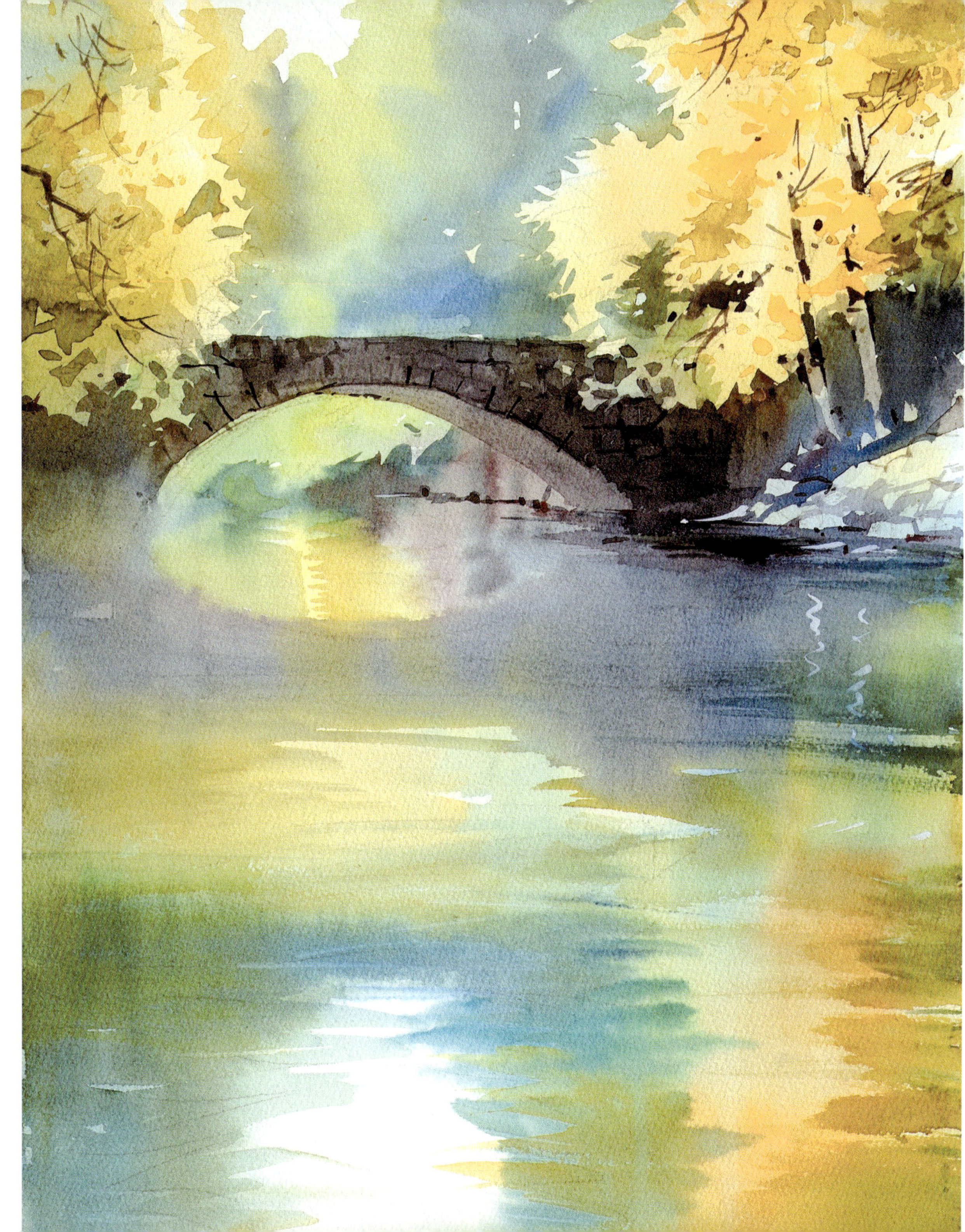

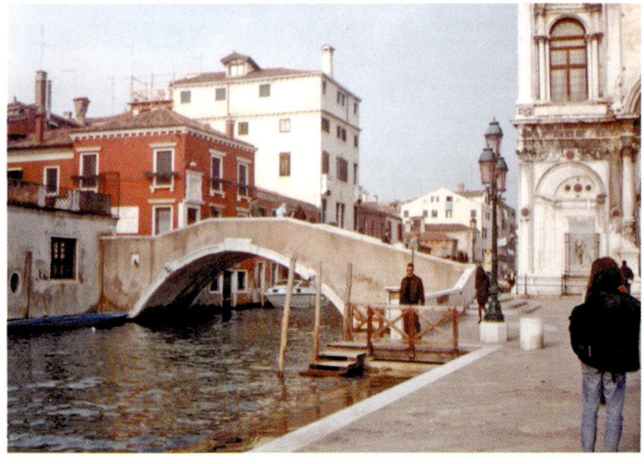

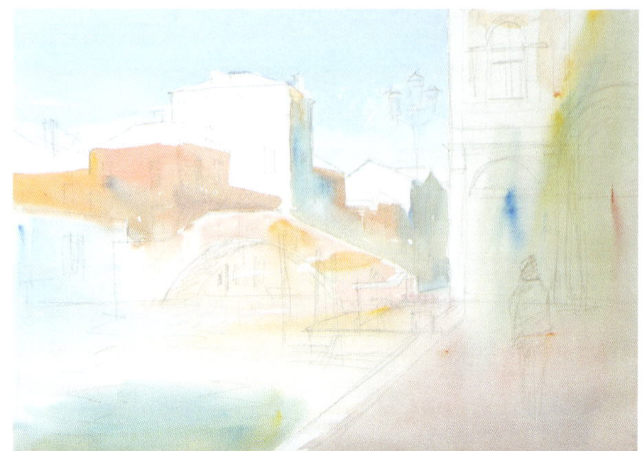

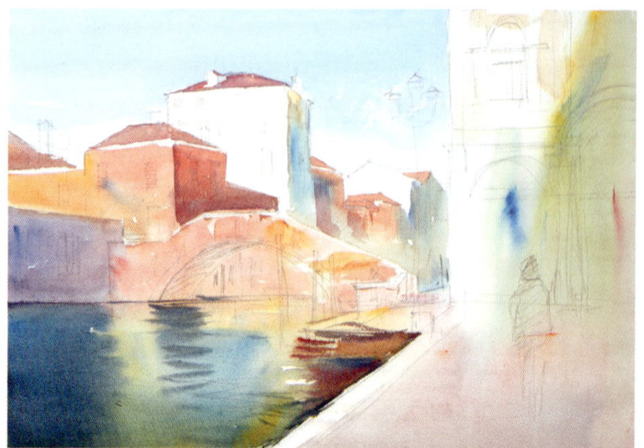

When we paint a scene, what is that we are expected to do? Obviously we are not going to paint each and every detail. What we are going to attempt is to present or bring out the beauty of a scene by a careful choice of colours, forms and their inter-relationship.

In the adjoining photograph, I chose not to paint the sharp edges of the buildings. I deliberately softened them. I tried to lead the viewer's eye into the painting and towards the point of attraction.

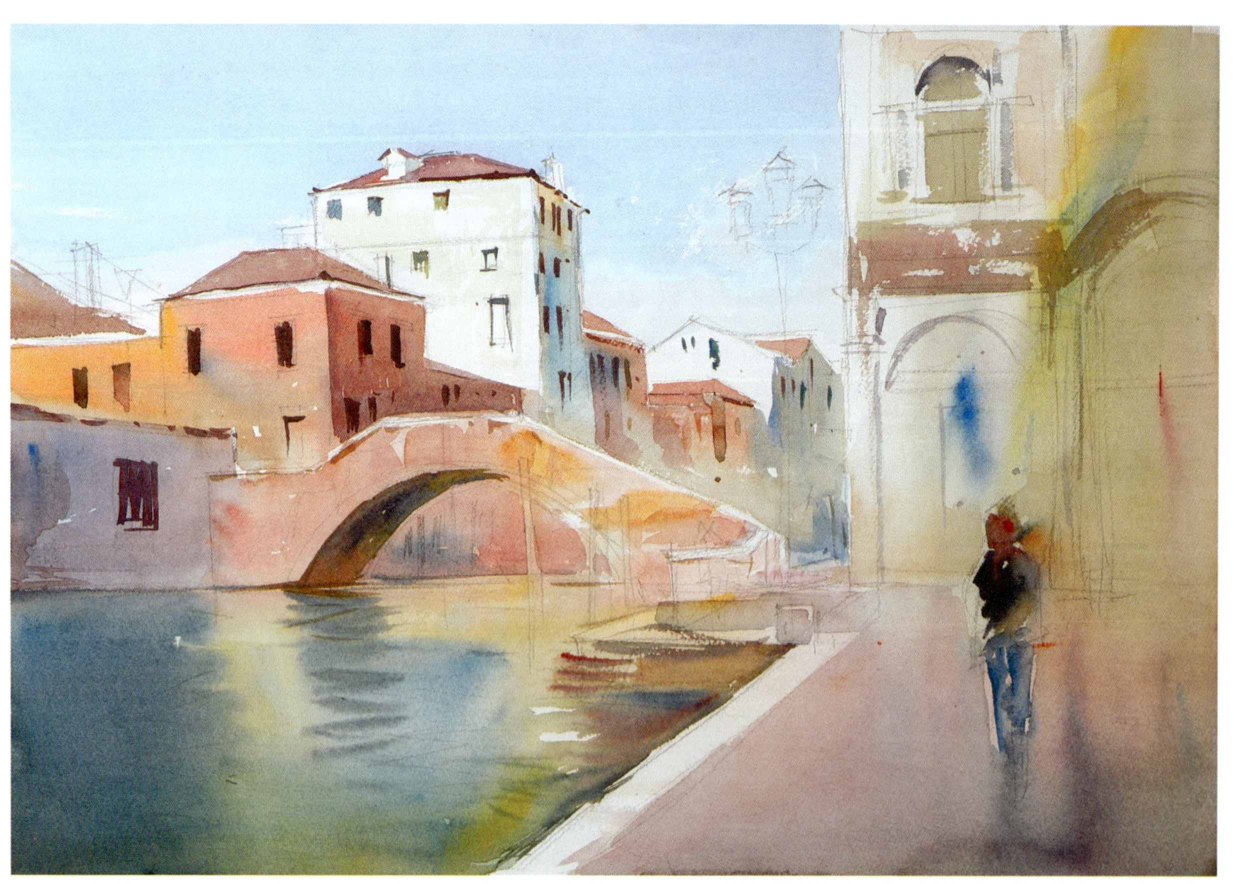

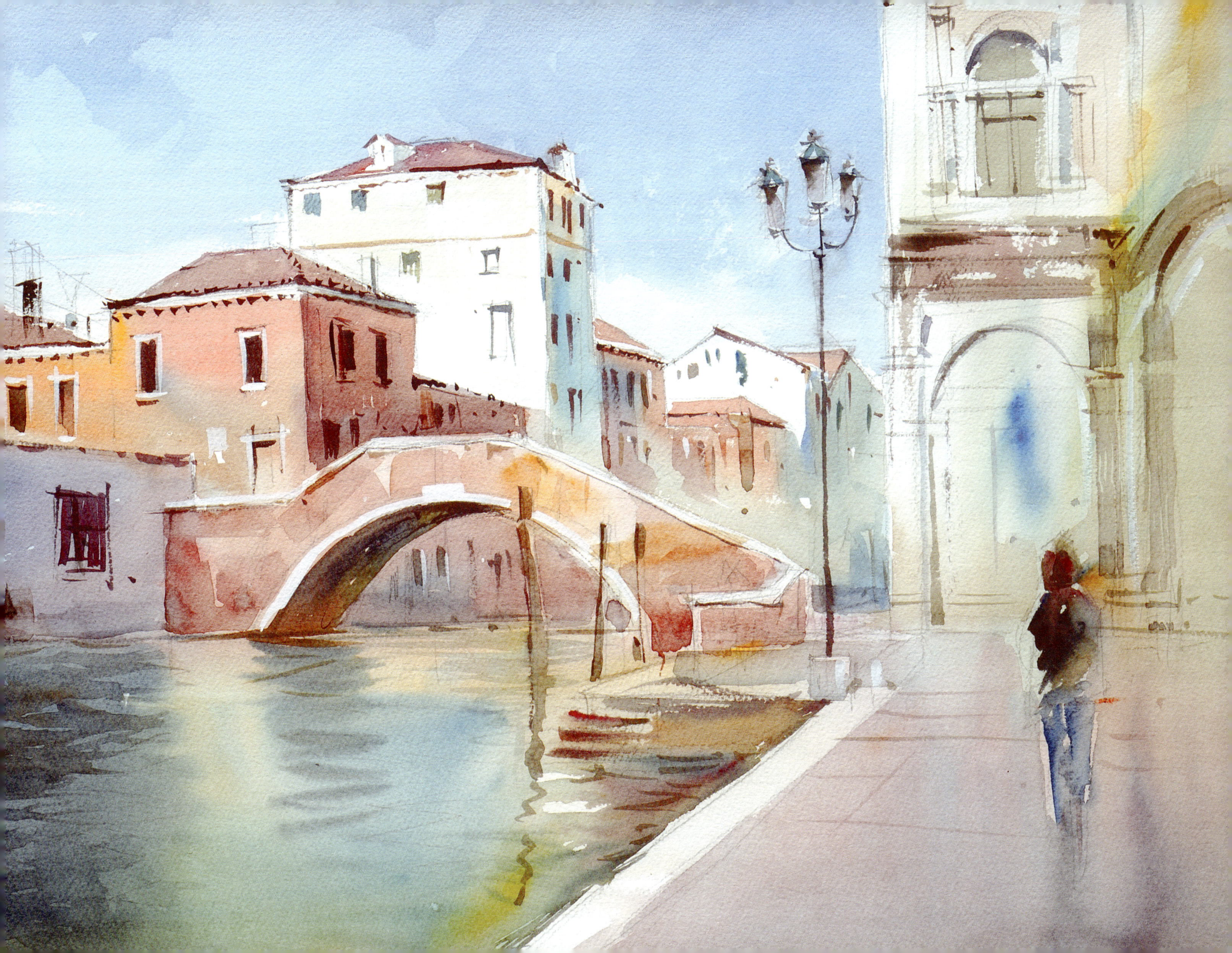

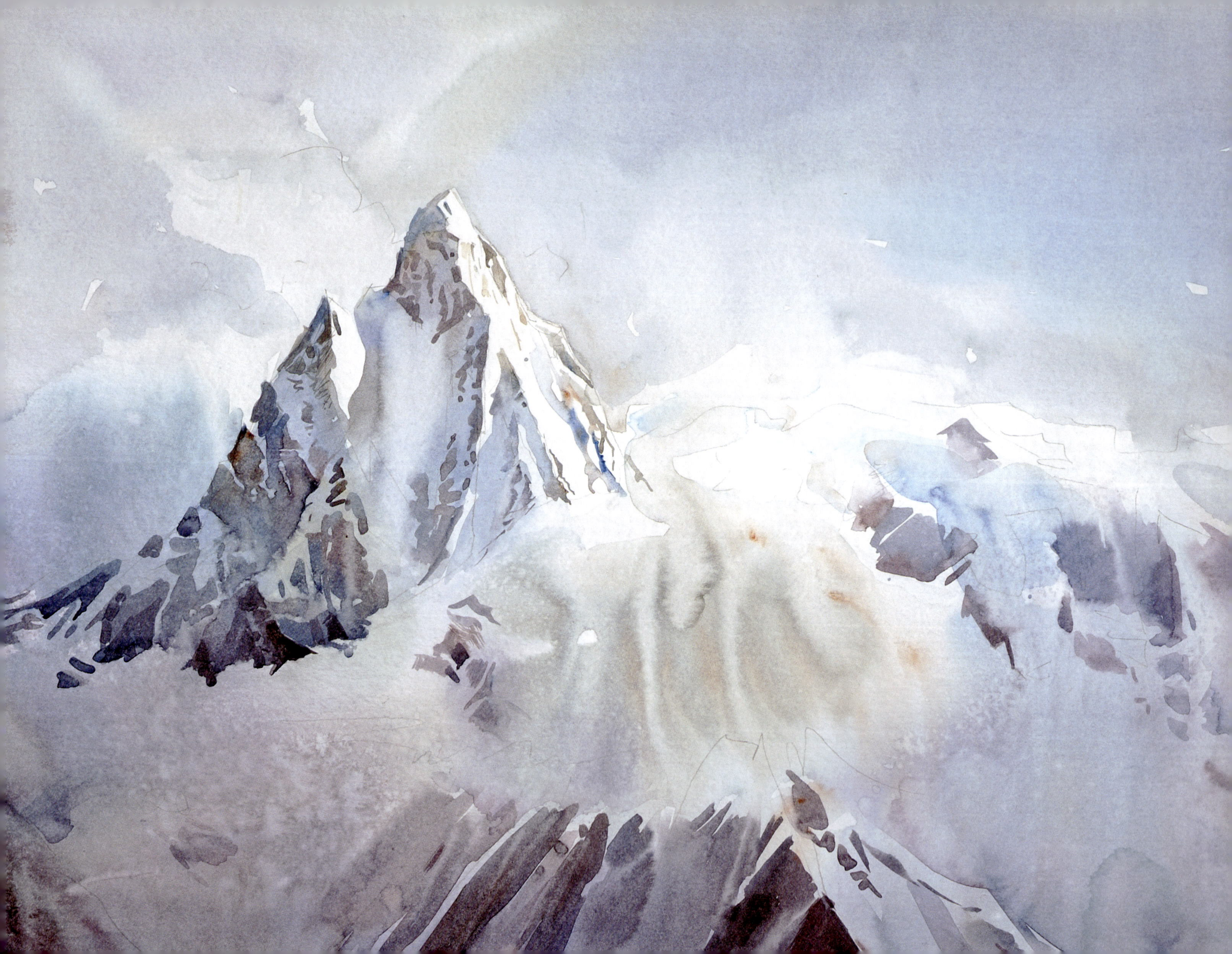

Assignment Twelve

Try out a painting using a photograph that you have liked. But see that it is a photograph that you have clicked. This will ensure that you remember the spot as well as the atmosphere there while painting. Without your realising it, all this will find its way into your work.

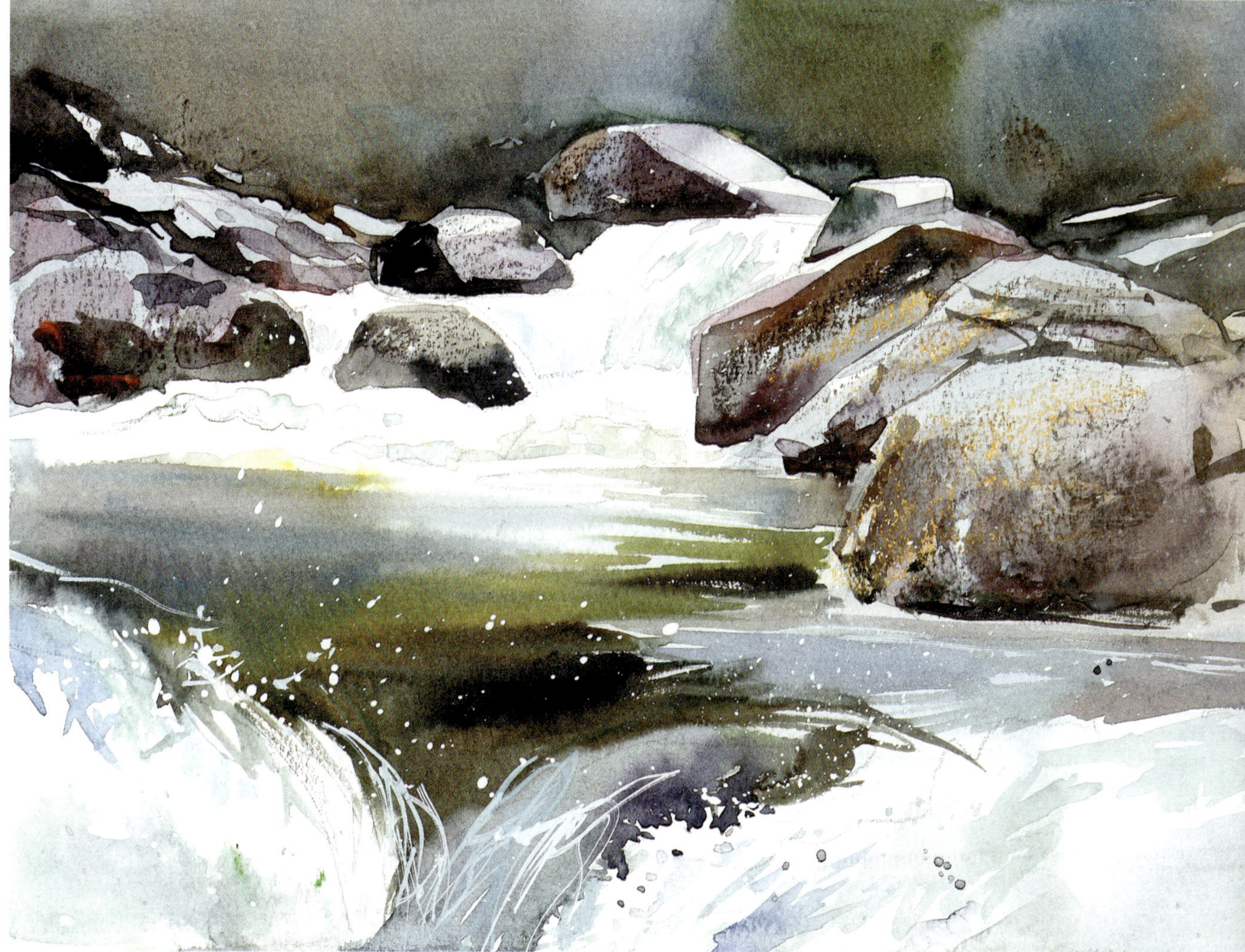

Whenever I paint a scene, I do not just paint all the elements in it. It is not a copy of what lies in front of me. The play of light and shadows, the atmosphere, my feelings at that time and the way my mind reacts to all these are vital in the painting process. In fact the painting is an amalgamation of all these factors. Among these, feelings have great importance. That is why, the same spot generates different paintings when painted at different times.

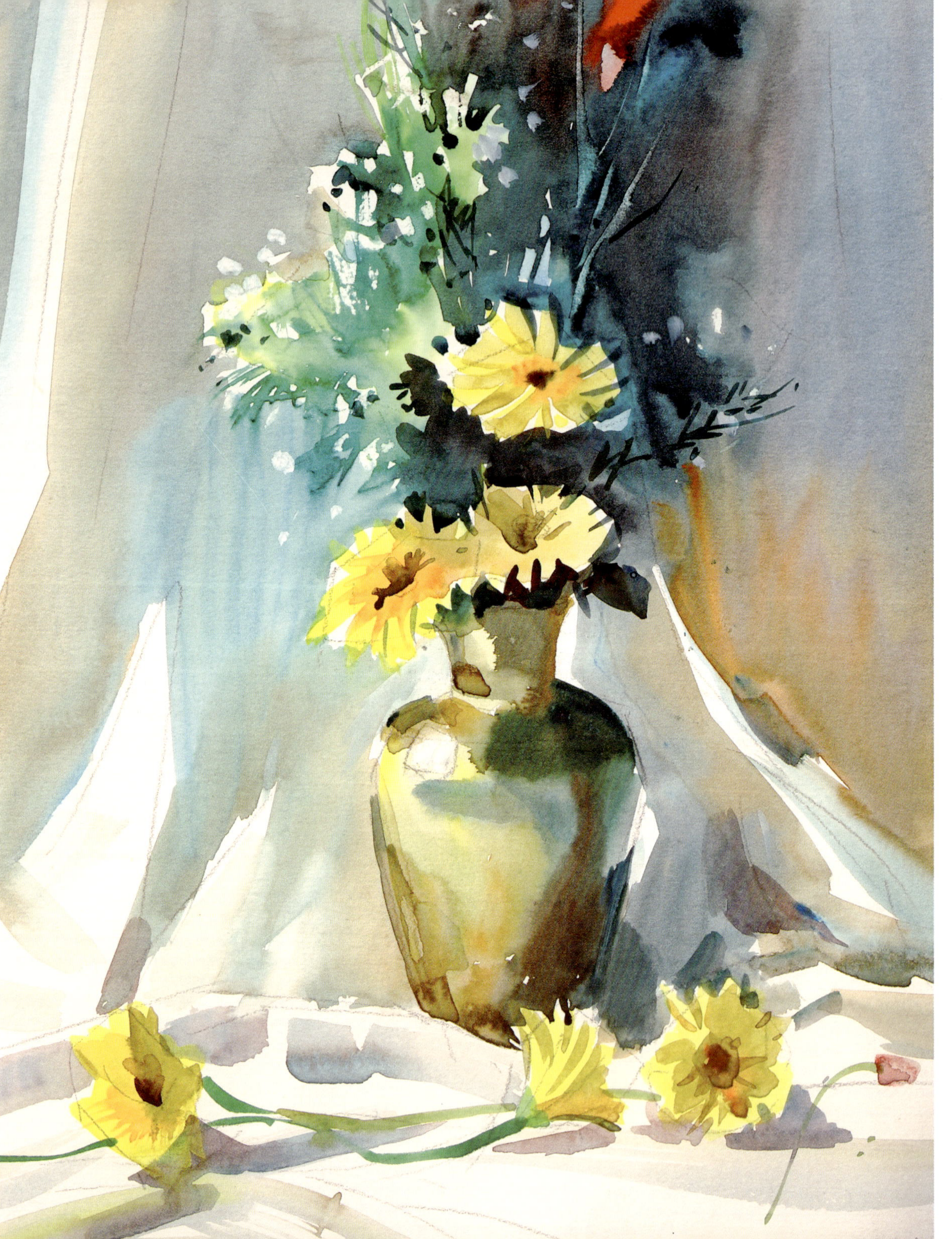

You have begun this exciting journey of watercolour painting. Through the demonstrations and assignments you have learnt the various techniques that are employed. We have also seen how to paint 'directly'.

As you explore the way ahead you will realize that techniques are the 'props' that hold your hands as you take the first tentative steps. But perhaps the real friends on your journey will be your interest and enthusiasm. So don't hold back. We have shown you the direction. Now it is up to you to get rid of your fears, shed your inhibitions and go ahead.

All the best!